Recommendations for Improving the Recruiting and Hiring of Los Angeles Firefighters

Chaitra M. Hardison, Nelson Lim, Kirsten M. Keller,
Jefferson P. Marquis, Leslie Adrienne Payne, Robert Bozick,
Louis T. Mariano, Jacqueline A. Mauro, Lisa Miyashiro,
Gillian Oak, Lisa Saum-Manning

For more information on this publication, visit www.rand.org/t/rr687

Library of Congress Cataloging-in-Publication Data is available for this publication.

ISBN: 978-0-8330-8839-0

Published by the RAND Corporation, Santa Monica, Calif.

© Copyright 2015 Los Angeles Fire Department

RAND® is a registered trademark.

Cover image: REUTERS/Jonathan Alcorn

www.rand.org

Preface

In 2014, the City of Los Angeles Mayor's Office sought assistance from the RAND Corporation to find ways to improve the process the city uses to hire firefighters into the Los Angeles Fire Department (LAFD). RAND proposed and received approval to execute a research and analysis project that has four primary goals:

- Recommend ways to improve the city's hiring policies and practices so that it may identify the applicants most likely to be successful firefighters.
- Ensure that the city provides an equal opportunity of being hired to all qualified applicants for firefighter positions.
- Suggest methods for improving the demographic diversity of new firefighter hires.
- Minimize costs for the city and its applicants.

RAND conducted a three-month review of Los Angeles's firefighter hiring policies and practices, paying particular attention to their effectiveness and fairness. This report presents the results of that three-month effort. It reviews the city's current hiring practices, outlines a new firefighter hiring process, and makes recommendations that are intended to increase efficiency of the hiring process, bolster the evidence supporting the validity of it, and make it more transparent and inclusive.

A Note About Hiring Practices and the Law

Although we discuss several aspects of employment law throughout this report, this is not intended to be legal advice or recommended strategy. Before proceeding with any changes to its selection process, the city should consult with its own legal counsel to determine an appropriate course of action.

The RAND Safety and Justice Program

The research reported here was conducted in the RAND Safety and Justice Program, which addresses all aspects of public safety and the criminal justice system, including violence, policing, corrections, courts and criminal law, substance abuse, occupational safety, and public integrity. Program research is supported by government agencies, foundations, and the private sector.

This program is part of RAND Justice, Infrastructure, and Environment, a division of the RAND Corporation dedicated to improving policy and decisionmaking in a wide range of policy domains, including civil and criminal justice, infrastructure protection and homeland security, transportation and energy policy, and environmental and natural resource policy. For more information about the Safety and Justice Program, see http://www.rand.org/safety-justice or contact the director at sj@rand.org.

Contents

Preface iii
Figures and Tables ix
Summary xi
Acknowledgments xxi
Abbreviations xxiii

CHAPTER ONE
Introduction 1
Scope and Limitations of This Report 2
  Time Constraints 2
  The City's Recent Changes 3
Objectives Guiding the Project 3
  Identify Applicants Most Likely to Be Successful Firefighters 4
  Ensure Equal Opportunity Throughout the Hiring Process 4
  Increase the Demographic Diversity of New Firefighter Hires 4
  Minimize Costs for the City of Los Angeles and Its Applicants 5
Study Approach 6
  Drawing on Existing Expertise and Past Research 6
  Exploratory Interviews to Understand Stakeholder Perspectives 9
  Review of Existing Documentation and Informational Interviews on
    Recruiting and Selection Processes 10
  Job Incumbent Focus Groups to Confirm and Identify New Key
    Duties, Knowledge, Skills, Abilities, and Other Characteristics
    for Firefighter Service 10
  Data Analyses to Examine Disparate Impact of the 2013 Selection
    Process 11
Organization of This Report 11

CHAPTER TWO
Firefighter Recruitment and Outreach Strategies 13
A Framework for Understanding Recruitment 13
Firefighter Recruiting Practices 14
Key Comments on Recruiting from the Interviews 16
The Emphasis Should Be on Finding Highly Qualified Candidates,
    Not Merely on Increasing the Quantity of Candidates 17

CHAPTER THREE
The 2013 Firefighter Selection Process 21
Notification Cards 23
Step 1: Preliminary Background Application 23
Step 2: Describing the Minimum Requirements 23
Step 3: Written Test 24
    Test of Reading Comprehension, Arithmetic, and Mechanical
        Aptitude 24
    Test Development 25
Step 4: Candidate Physical Ability Test 26
Step 5: Oral Interview 27
    Job Interview with a Firefighter and Interview Specialist 27
Step 6: Background Investigation and Preliminary Investigative
    Questionnaire 29
    Collection of Preliminary Background Information Using
        Applicant-Provided Information 29
Step 7: Initial Panel Review 30
    Two Fire Captains Review the Candidate's Initial Background
        Application Package. 30
Step 8: Field Investigation 32
    In-Depth Background Check 32
Step 9: Final Panel Review 33
    Repeat of Initial Panel Review with Corroborated Information 33
Step 10: Medical and Psychological Evaluations 33
Certification 34

CHAPTER FOUR
Statistical Analysis of the Selection Process 35
Data 35
Reduction of Applicants in the Selection Process.......................... 36
The Selection Process's Impact on Minorities 39
Caution in Interpreting These Estimates Is Warranted..................... 42

CHAPTER FIVE
Recommendations 45
Overview of Recommendations as They Relate to the Objectives 46
  Objective 1: Identify Applicants Most Likely to Be Successful
    Firefighters... 46
  Objective 2: Ensure Equal Opportunity Throughout the
    Hiring Process... 48
  Objective 3: Increase the Demographic Diversity of New
    Firefighter Hires...49
  Objective 4: Minimize Costs for the City of Los Angeles and Its
    Applicants...49
Overarching Recommendations Targeting the Four Objectives 50
  Start a New Citywide Outreach and Recruiting Campaign for
    the LAFD.. 50
  Validate Selection Criteria by Establishing Relationships to KSAOs
    Required to Be an Effective Firefighter................................55
  Explore Options for Reducing the Applicant Pool to a
    Manageable Size.. 56
  Establish a Robust Appeals Process for Applicants Who Believe
    That They Have Been Wrongly Deselected 64
  Increase Electronic Documentation and Use of Online Technology
    During the Selection Process 65
  Align the Content in Each Selection Step with the Job Analysis
    and Deconflict It with Other Elements in the Process.............. 66
  Tie Minimums on All Selection Factors to Acceptable and
    Unacceptable Performance in Training or on the Job.................67
Step-by-Step Recommendations for Improving the Selection Process...... 67
  Suggested Changes to Step 1: Preliminary Background Application
    and Step 2: Minimum Requirements 68

Suggested Changes to Step 3: Written Test...................................71
Suggested Changes to Step 4: Candidate Physical Ability Test...........73
Suggested Changes to Step 5: Oral Interview, Step 6: Background
    Investigation and Preliminary Investigative Questionnaire,
    and Step 8: Field Investigation 74
Suggested Changes to Step 7: Initial Panel Review and Step 9:
    Final Panel Review...78
Suggested Changes to Step 10: Medical and Psychological
    Evaluations..78

APPENDIXES
A. Key Considerations in Evaluating the Selection Process 81
**B. Defining Critical Firefighter Tasks, Knowledge, Skills,
    Abilities, and Other Characteristics**................................... 91
C. Outsourcing the Written Test for Entry-Level Firefighters 99
**D. The Impact of Chance Variability in Simple Random
    Sampling** 105
**E. Mathematics and Examples of Key Considerations for
    Stratified Sampling** 111

References 119

Figures and Tables

Figures

2.1. Factors Influencing the Number and Diversity of LAFD
Firefighter Recruits 14
2.2. Los Angeles County Population (Census Data) 18
2.3. Firefighter Applicants Meeting Minimum Requirements 19
3.1. Timeline of 2013 Firefighter Selection Process................. 22
4.1. 1,000 Hypothetical Applicants Retained and Lost
Through Firefighter Evaluation and Investigation
Strategies... 38
D.1. Probability Intervals for the Percentage of Whites in a
Random Sample from an Applicant Pool That Is
50.34 Percent White.. 107
D.2. Probability Intervals for the Percentage of Males in a
Random Sample from an Applicant Pool That Is
94.30 Percent Male... 108

Tables

1.1. Stakeholder Interviewees... 9
4.1. Number and Percentage Moving on at Each Selection
Step, 2013 Applicant Cohort 37
4.2. Ethnic and Gender Differences in Rates of Passing Each
Step of the Firefighter Evaluation and Investigation
Process, 2013 Applicant Cohort 41

4.3. Number and Percentage Taking Versus Passing the
      Written Test, 2013 Applicant Cohort 43
4.4. Ethnic and Gender Differences in Rates of Passing the
      CPAT at the Orange County Testing Center,
      January 1, 2013–April 21, 2013 43
5.1. Suggested Alternative Firefighter Hiring Processes for
      the LAFD... 69
5.2. Factors Evaluated in the Background Investigations and
      Interviews 77
B.1. Competencies Documented in 2010 and Reinforced in
      RAND Focus Groups.. 94
B.2. Suggestions for Expanding the List of Firefighter
      Duty Tasks 95
C.1. Ergometrics... 102
C.2. CWH Management Solutions 103
C.3. I/O Solutions... 104
E.1. Stratified Sampling Example, In Which 3 Percent of
      Each Sub-Population Is Selected............................... 113

Summary

In 2013, after a five-year hiring freeze, the City of Los Angeles resumed hiring new firefighters for the Los Angeles Fire Department (LAFD). Within a year, however, the hiring effort was met with waves of criticism and calls for reform.[1] Critics charged, among other things, that the selection criteria lacked transparency and that the hiring process appeared to favor applicants with connections to current LAFD firefighters. They argued that the training class was significantly less racially diverse than the city of Los Angeles and contained only one female candidate. They also cited that more than 20 percent of the recruits were relatives of LAFD firefighters.

In response to the criticism and calls for reform, Los Angeles Mayor Eric Garcetti suspended the firefighter hiring process before the next group of recruits could begin training. The LAFD began an internal investigation, and the Mayor's Office approached the RAND Corporation for assistance in recommending ways to improve the firefighter hiring process. In response, RAND conducted a three-month review of Los Angeles's hiring policies and practices for firefighters.

This report describes this review and presents recommendations on ways the city could more effectively manage its pool of firefighter applicants and revise its hiring process.

---

[1] For background on the criticism, see Welsh and Lopez, 2014; Lopez and Welsh, 2014a, 2014b; Lopez, Zahniser, and Welsh, 2014; Orlov, 2014; and Lloyd, 2014.

Scope and Limitations of This Report

The three-month time frame limited the scope of our review, findings, and recommendations. It afforded us enough time to review the existing approaches for selecting firefighters and any existing evidence supporting the selection process, but it did not permit the collection of new data to validate the usefulness of that process. As a result, many of our recommendations suggest conducting additional data collection and research (including conducting validation studies) that could not be undertaken during the time frame of this study.

Objectives

At the outset of the project, RAND and the LAFD agreed that to improve its hiring process the LAFD should strive to achieve at least four overarching objectives:

1. Identify applicants most likely to be successful firefighters.
2. Ensure equal opportunity throughout the hiring process.
3. Increase the demographic diversity of new LAFD firefighter hires.
4. Minimize costs for the city of Los Angeles and applicants.

Study Approach

To address these objectives a multidisciplinary team of RAND researchers executed a research plan to perform qualitative and quantitative analysis of the firefighter hiring process: This plan was designed to

- Better understand firefighter recruiting and outreach efforts. We reviewed existing documentation on the city's efforts and conducted interviews with members of the LAFD's Recruit Services Section and other key stakeholders.

- Document and assess the inherent duties and knowledge, skills, abilities, and other characteristics (KSAOs) needed to successfully perform the job of firefighter at the LAFD. To that end, we
  - reviewed a broad range of literature on firefighter job requirements
  - reviewed an unpublished 1994 job analysis study conducted by the City of Los Angeles Personnel Department's Research Section and a related 2010 update, also unpublished, that was conducted by a private-sector firm
  - conducted focus group interviews to confirm and supplement the KSAOs identified in 1994 and 2010.
- Gain a better understanding of the current firefighter selection process. This involved
  - reviewing existing documentation on the process and meeting with Personnel Department staff to better understand each step in the selection process
  - analyzing quantitative data on firefighter applicants to better understand the demographic impact of the selection process on the diversity of the firefighter applicants and selectees.

Findings

LAFD's Recruitment and Outreach Strategies

Outreach and recruitment fall within the purview of the Recruitment Unit—a subset of the LAFD's Recruit Services Section. The four individuals who make up this unit attend job fairs and community events and conduct school visitations. Individual firefighters also often assist with these activities on their off days.

Four youth fire academies in the greater Los Angeles area strive to equip youth with life skills and professional guidance, in addition to teaching them the ins-and-outs of firefighting. These academies often serve as precursors to the Cadet Program, which functions as an internship that introduces youth to the culture and expectations of the LAFD.

LAFD personnel and stakeholders we interviewed felt that a lack of sufficient funds and available personnel significantly impacts the time, resources, and effort invested in firefighter outreach and recruitment, and that expanding the recruiting budget and staff would favorably impact outreach and recruiting efforts across Los Angeles. Our interviewees reported a belief that some members of minority groups, and women especially, have had a lower propensity to apply for firefighter positions compared with white males, but that improving the diversity of the applicant pool is possible with a long-term outreach and recruitment campaign.

The City's Current Selection Process

Based on documentation from the Personnel Department and interviews with its staff, we obtained details on the ten-step process of selecting firefighters used by the city in 2013. These are provided in Chapter Three.

Statistical Analysis of the Selection Process

Using data from the 2013 cohort of applicants, we identified steps in the process (1) that eliminated a large proportion of the applicants and (2) that had disparate impact on the racial, ethnic, and gender representation of the applicant pool. We found the following:

- Most applicants who met the minimum eligibility requirements were eliminated by either the written exam portion of the firefighter selection process or the requirement to submit their Candidate Physical Ability Test (CPAT) certification within a specific time window. (Firefighter applicants are required to pass the CPAT, which is administered by an external organization, the California Fire Fighter Joint Apprentice Committee. In 2013, candidates could submit their CPAT certification starting at 8:00 a.m., April 22, 2013. Due to an overwhelming number of respondents, only those applicants who submitted their certification in the first minute after 8:00 a.m. were permitted to continue in the hiring process.)

- A larger proportion of Hispanic, black, and female applicants failed to take and pass the written test portion of the selection process, relative to white male applicants.
- A larger proportion of Hispanic, black, Asian, and female applicants failed to submit their CPAT certification within the required time window, relative to white male applicants.
- According to data from the organization that administers the CPAT, 94 percent of the people who take the test pass it. Hence, the CPAT itself does not eliminate many applicants.

Recommendations

We offer several recommendations on how the city can achieve the four objectives listed above. These include making specific revisions to the firefighter selection process.

Start a Citywide Firefighter Outreach and Recruiting Campaign

Recent negative media coverage of the firefighter selection process may have exacerbated perceptions that the city is not committed to improving diversity. Starting a new recruiting and outreach effort targeting highly qualified minority and female candidates is a good first step to improving some of those negative public perceptions.

For example, the city could reach out to specific highly qualified individuals who would add to the LAFD's demographic diversity, such as female athletes at local colleges or members of minority groups who are recent military veterans. In addition, the city could consider using fire stations as outreach and recruiting centers to target the communities they serve. If the city chooses to use fire stations in this way, its Personnel Department should consider providing in-depth training to some members of fire stations on what they can and cannot say as part of the hiring process and certifying them as official recruiters.

Enhancing outreach and recruitment can also be done by expanding the capabilities of the firefighter recruiting website (http://www.joinlafd.org/). For example, the website could be used to monitor trends in individuals who are interested in applying for firefighter positions or to accept applications online and automate the initial screening process. The website may have some capability to do some of this monitoring and screening already.

Validate Selection Criteria by Establishing Relationships to the KSAOs Required to Be an Effective Firefighter

We found that many elements of the current firefighting hiring process are consistent with best practices of personnel selection. However, additional validation efforts can strengthen the link between selection criteria being used and required KSAOs. Depending on the types of criteria, the validation methods can vary. For instance, the Personnel Department should assemble a panel of subject-matter experts and stakeholders to establish behavioral criteria that can be used to disqualify or non-select personnel during the official background investigation.[2] The panel should also review and approve behavioral dimensions that background investigators and interviewers use to evaluate applicants in the selection process. All selection criteria should be aligned with one another and with the required KSAOs. The Personnel Department should validate (or have outside experts validate) all qualifying tests used in the selection process. In addition, the interview and background investigation portions of the selection process should be designed to provide a good assessment of skills easily tapped using those methodologies (such as interpersonal skills, illegal behaviors, or other abilities and personal characteristics identified in the job analysis). Steps should be taken to validate those portions of the process as well.

---

[2] Note that this would be a substantial change to the process as explicit minimum disqualifying or non-selection criteria do not currently exist for the background investigation information. Additionally, all people who are officially disqualified (as opposed to non-selected) must be afforded an opportunity to appeal the process. Such appeals could increase the burden placed on the city if the criteria were used for disqualification rather than non-selection. Although this too would be a substantial change to the firefighter selection process, by establishing explicit criteria for non-selection or disqualification, final results for individuals would likely be much more replicable, defensible, and transparent.

Explore Options for Reducing the Applicant Pool to a Manageable Size

In 2013, the number of firefighter applicants to the city dwarfed the number of available positions. When the number of applicants becomes excessive the Personnel Department cannot allow everyone to move through the selection process. Instead, the department uses a multiple-hurdle system in which only those who pass a given hurdle are allowed to continue on to the next step in the screening process. In 2013, this approach resulted in disparate impact for key demographic groups.[3] Therefore, the department should reevaluate the processes it uses to winnow down the number of applicants to a manageable size. In doing so, the city should pay particular attention to disparate impact (i.e., whether these processes affect the diversity of the applicant pool) and the validity of the tool and the minimums used in that winnowing process.

There is no obvious answer for how best to winnow the applicant pool. We discuss two options, each of which has advantages and disadvantages:[4]

- **Top-down selection on the written test.** If the Personnel Department had evidence that scores on the test relate to higher performance in job-related situations, it could select people in order of their scores to narrow the applicant pool to a manageable level. This is a merit-based approach known as top-down selection. However, the use of such a test could result in disparate impact against some demographic groups. If this approach is used and the test shows disparate impact, we recommend that the Personnel Department consider adding a non-cognitive-personality

---

[3] See Chapter Four.

[4] Legal issues should be factored into the decision of which method is most appropriate (see Appendix A for more discussion on this). Those legal issues are constantly evolving. Recent court cases involving aptitude tests that show disparate impact have new complexities. Moreover, it is not clear how random selection practices would be received by the courts. We therefore recommend that the city's legal counsel advise them on which, if any, of these options is advisable in the current legal environment. See Appendix A for more discussion on this.

measure to the written test and use a combined score for top-down selection. This can help maintain greater diversity within the applicant pool (as personality tests often do not show disparate impact) and provide a more well-rounded assessment of the applicants. We also would recommend targeted recruiting aimed at finding and attracting minority applicants who are likely to be highly competitive on the aptitude test. Doing so would serve to lower the observed disparate impact of the test for those groups.

- **Random sampling.** To help increase the probability that minority representation is maintained in the applicant pool, the city might consider using random sampling (either simple random sampling or stratified random sampling) rather than aptitude testing to narrow the initially very large applicant pool to a manageable level. This approach would help preserve the diversity of the initial applicant pool, and it could be used in combination with a careful, rigorous, and valid applicant screening process to ensure that only highly qualified candidates receive offers, consistent with the fact that public safety is the primary desired outcome of firefighter hiring. However, we are aware of only one large metropolitan fire department currently using random selection as part of its hiring process. Although that organization plans to continue to use random selection in future hiring cycles, two other departments that have tried it in the past reported that it was not viewed favorably by many of the applicants.

The approaches are not mutually exclusive, and an effective selection process might involve a combination of both approaches.

Whichever approach or combination of approaches is used, the Personnel Department should take care in determining the size of the pool that continues in the selection process. Over-reducing the number of applicants early on in the process could result in too few applicants later on, in which case standards and expectations might have to be lowered in order to have enough selectees at the end of the selection process. To prevent that from occurring, we suggest that the Personnel Department seek to maximize the size of the applicant pool deemed "manageable." We also recommend that checks be in place to make sure that the resulting pool stays highly competitive in the later hurdles.

Set Aside Funding and Resources for a Robust Appeals Process for Applicants Who Believe That They Have Been Wrongly Passed Over

Having robust appeals procedures for applicants who believe they have been treated unfairly during the selection process or believe they were not selected because of some bias in the system will build trust in the firefighter hiring process and minimize chances for costly litigations. The firefighter recruiting website should post information about the appeals process.[5] This should include the necessary information to submit to initiate appeals and clear guidelines on how individual applicants can better meet selection criteria.

Improve the Firefighter Selection Process Through a Variety of Specific Revisions

The city's current personnel selection practices are generally consistent with best practices in personnel selection. However, the process could be improved. In Chapter Five, we offer specific suggestions for improving the selection process, such as conducting electronic background checks earlier in the process, identifying overlaps in content among selection processes, outsourcing the written test to a private vendor, and further standardizing interview and background investigation processes. In general, our suggestions are intended to promote transparency in the selection process, manage applicants' expectations, and help to identify viable and competitive applicants early in the process so as to improve efficiency and save resources for both the city and its applicants. The suggestions can also provide additional theoretical and empirical support for the reliability and validity of selection practices, two key elements in ensuring legal defensibility.

---

[5]   Note that there is an appeals process for candidates who fail parts of the application process. The only part of the process not appealable is the panel review processes, because instead of a "fail" result or disqualification, candidates are non-selected if they are not the most competitive. The city has noted that resources would be a big concern if appeals for panel review were implemented.

Acknowledgments

We could not have conducted this review of the Los Angeles Fire Department hiring process without generous assistance from dedicated staff of the City of Los Angeles. We are grateful to the many LAFD firefighters, fire captains, and fire chiefs who contributed their time, attention, and expertise to this study despite their demanding work schedules. Their willingness to share their expertise and knowledge provided an invaluable layer of context and substance to RAND's research efforts. Relatedly, we extend our thanks and appreciation to the LAFD's Fire Commission, which availed itself to our research team and provided valuable insight into the department and its entry-level selection process. The assistance provided by the City of Los Angeles Personnel Department is especially appreciated. In particular, we recognize Margaret Whelan, General Manager of the Personnel Department; Gloria Sosa, Assistant General Manager of the Personnel Department; the Chief of the Selection Division; the Chief of the Public Safety Background Division; and the Firefighter Examination Analyst. Last, but certainly not least, we extend a very special thanks to Drew Steinberg of the Mayor's Office of Homeland Security and Public Safety for tirelessly assisting the RAND study team in scheduling its many interviews and meetings.

We would also like to express sincere gratitude to several others who contributed in various ways to the completion of the final report. We thank Geoffrey McGovern, who contributed his expertise to early drafts of the report, and Gordon Lee, James Torr, Kelly Schwartz, and Melissa Bauman, who worked tirelessly providing expert communication and editorial assistance on numerous drafts. We also greatly appreciate the timely and insightful comments and feedback provided by our reviewers, Laura S. Hamilton, Anita Chandra, and Debra L. Schroeder of RAND and Assistant Chief Alan D. Vickery of the Seattle Fire Department.

Abbreviations

CPAT	Candidate Physical Ability Test
CWH	CWH Management Solutions
DMV	Department of Motor Vehicles
EMT	emergency medical technician
IRB	institutional review board
KSAO	knowledge, skills, abilities, and other characteristics
LAFD	Los Angeles Fire Department
MMPI	Minnesota Multiphasic Personality Inventory
O*NET	Occupational Information Network
PIQ	Preliminary Investigative Questionnaire
PHF	Personal History Form

CHAPTER ONE

Introduction

In 2013, after a five-year hiring freeze, the City of Los Angeles resumed hiring new firefighters for the Los Angeles Fire Department (LAFD). Within a year, however, the hiring effort was met with waves of criticism and calls for reform.[1] Critics charged, among other things, that the selection criteria lacked transparency and that the hiring process appeared to favor applicants with connections to current LAFD firefighters. They argued that the training class was significantly less racially diverse than the city of Los Angeles and contained only one female candidate. They also cited the fact that more than 20 percent of the recruits were relatives of LAFD firefighters.

Many detractors directed specific criticism at what they called the city's alleged unannounced "first come, first served" application process, in which applicants who failed to submit evidence of passing the department's required physical fitness test during the crush of submissions in the first 60 seconds of the filing period were not permitted to continue on in the process. Although this process was criticized heavily, the LAFD job bulletin announced that candidates would be processed in the order that their Candidate Physical Ability Test (CPAT) certification was received.[2]

In response to the criticism and calls for reform, Los Angeles Mayor Eric Garcetti suspended the firefighter hiring process before

---

[1] For background on the criticism, see Welsh and Lopez, 2014; Lopez and Welsh, 2014a, 2014b; Lopez, Zahniser, and Welsh, 2014; Orlov, 2014; and Lloyd, 2014.

[2] This process was intended to help the city manage the overwhelming number of applicants it received.

the next group of recruits could begin training. The LAFD began an internal investigation, and the Mayor's Office approached the RAND Corporation for assistance in recommending ways to improve the firefighter hiring process. Maintaining performance standards, ensuring fairness, improving diversity, and keeping costs to a minimum were among the goals expressed for an improved process.

To address the request, RAND conducted a three-month review of the Los Angeles recruiting and hiring policies and practices for firefighters. The primary goal was to provide short-term and immediate recommendations for changes that could be made to improve the selection process.

Scope and Limitations of This Report

Time Constraints

The city asked RAND to provide within 90 days recommendations for changes to the selection process. As a result, the work reflected in this report to support those recommendations had to be scoped to fit that time constraint.

RAND limited its approach to reviewing existing documentation on the current selection process and meeting with stakeholders and the City of Los Angeles Personnel Department to better understand the key issues they faced. During the first month, we received approvals from the RAND institutional review board (IRB) to contact members of the Personnel Department, stakeholders, and subject-matter experts to learn more about the selection process, and to review relevant data and past research supporting it. During the second month, we held discussions and interviews with members of those groups. We requested approvals from the IRB to obtain applicant data and conduct focus groups with firefighters confirming the job analysis information provided to us during our initial interviews with the Personnel Department. During both months, we contacted testing firms, conducted searches of existing literature, and contacted other fire departments to obtain as much information as we could to make our recommendations. Data cleaning and analysis and report writing, followed by the research quality assurance and peer-review process required of all RAND publications, were condensed into month three.

Because of the short time frame, we did not have time to go back to the city to ask for additional data or to conduct additional interviews. This would routinely be done on studies with longer turnaround times. We instead acknowledge these time constraints as limitations to the work. The recommendations discussed here are based only on the information we could obtain during the 90 days. More research, data, and interviews would be ideal for making recommended changes to any selection process. As a result, many of our recommendations include conducting additional research and data collection to provide support for the existing processes.

The City's Recent Changes

RAND was asked to evaluate the selection process that was in place when the study was initiated in 2014. That selection process was the same as that used in the 2013 hiring cycle. However, prior to the deadline for submitting this study's recommendations, the city announced new changes to the selection process. It is therefore worth noting that the review and recommendations presented here cover the selection process prior to that change.

Objectives Guiding the Project

The project has four overarching objectives. While they are not an exhaustive list of objectives that could be relevant for the LAFD, they are the ones the city, stakeholders, and the Personnel Department targeted at the outset of this study. (See the section below describing the stakeholder interviews used to help confirm the relevance of these objectives.) Additionally, they are consistent with objectives commonly espoused by many organizations and objectives commonly discussed at length in the research literature on personnel selection.

Identify Applicants Most Likely to Be Successful Firefighters

The main priority of any municipality's effort to recruit and hire firefighters is to identify and attract individuals who have the knowledge, skills, abilities, and other characteristics (KSAOs) to be good firefighters. Fire departments need individuals who can fight fires, handle a range of contingencies, respond to medical emergencies, and manage an array of other public crises. Additionally, Los Angeles residents need to have confidence that firefighters—who at any moment may be tasked with running into residents' burning homes, handling their belongings, or saving their lives—are trustworthy protectors of their loved ones and valuables. In other words, fire departments above all else need individuals who can be good first responders.

Ensure Equal Opportunity Throughout the Hiring Process

Municipalities need to put in place policies, practices, and procedures ensuring that job applicants are treated fairly and placed on an equal playing field throughout the hiring process. This holds true not just for individuals vying for firefighter openings but for all who seek competitive civil service positions. It is a basic tenet of U.S. law and public service that applicants be given equal opportunity to demonstrate their capability to meet job-related requirements, and public agencies need to devise processes that are legally defensible.

Increase the Demographic Diversity of New Firefighter Hires

Los Angeles is one of the most demographically diverse communities in the United States and is becoming increasingly so with each passing year. Diversity is argued to be a valuable goal because having employees with diverse perspectives and backgrounds can help broaden the perspectives of an organization. Fostering diversity is also a way to help address concerns about social justice and in many cases demonstrate that instances of discrimination are in the past. Even performance-related reasons can support a desire to have a diverse workforce. For example, having a diverse workforce can help fire crews more easily communicate with non-English speakers during emergencies. Moreover, if the level of trust that the city's residents have for the fire department is at all affected by perceptions of the department's sensitivity to diversity, then having a diverse workforce becomes a social justice goal and may also improve the department's ability to ensure public safety. For other examples of why organizations might value a diverse workforce, see Robinson and Dechant (1997). Given the value of diversity, it is reasonable for the LAFD to ask, "How can we improve the diversity of our workforce?"

Minimize Costs for the City of Los Angeles[3] and Its Applicants

Los Angeles, like virtually all other municipalities in the country, is looking for ways to minimize costs and streamline operations. But that objective can sometimes be challenged when cities encounter certain realities of public sector hiring. Specifically, the LAFD, like fire departments in other large metropolitan areas, traditionally has a large number of applicants for a small number of job openings. In the LAFD's most recent firefighter hiring cycle, for example, 13,236 applicants filled out the preliminary background application to apply for 70 open training slots.[4] As a result, only 0.5 percent of the applicants could receive conditional job offers.

This large number of applicants far exceeds what the Personnel Department can handle. Some steps in the current hiring process, such as interviews and background investigations, are costly and time-consuming. With such a large number of applicants, the hiring process generates much higher costs than the city should reasonably be expected to shoulder.

At the same time, applicants face significant costs. They have to pay to complete the CPAT and to travel to testing sites (which for some individuals may be a one- or two-hour drive away). And they must wait months for answers about their applications, during which time many applicants may be postponing or passing up other job opportunities. And again, even the best-qualified candidates face low odds of being selected by the LAFD because of the limited number of available

---

[3] Although minimizing costs is an important goal, note that some efforts to reduce costs may be at odds with the objective of increasing diversity or recruiting individuals most likely to be successful firefighters.

[4] This level of interest is consistent with interest levels in other large metropolitan areas.

positions. These costs and wait times can be especially burdensome for applicants with limited resources.

Study Approach

To address these four objectives, a multidisciplinary team of RAND researchers executed a research plan that included qualitative as well as quantitative analysis of the firefighter hiring process. We explored some of the LAFD's firefighter recruiting and outreach efforts, identified key duties and KSAOs of members of the fire service, reviewed the firefighter selection process, and estimated the impact of selection stages on the demographic diversity of the applicant pool.

Drawing on Existing Expertise and Past Research

As noted above, RAND was asked to conduct a review of the city's existing selection practices and suggest changes. Typically, changes to selection processes are made *after* data and evidence supporting the validity of the selection procedures have been amassed. That is, changes to selection processes should not be implemented until they have been validated. Validation includes research showing that the selection practices are effective at predicting important outcomes. Validation may also include systematically documenting the links between the selection tools and requirements of the job. However, collection of such data would have required more time than was available for this study. The city instead asked RAND to provide answers in the near term using our existing knowledge of well-established recommended practices.

As a result, in addition to data collected directly from the city's firefighters and firefighter applicants, the recommendations we make in this report draw on findings and knowledge from our past work in personnel selection and workforce diversity issues. For example, our recommendations regarding recruiting practices and initiatives for improving diversity draw from our past and ongoing work in recruiting and diversity initiatives in the military, police, and civilian sectors. And our recommendations regarding changes to the selection practices draw from our past work in personnel selection. This includes work in test design and validation, measurement and prediction of performance, psychological measurement, evaluation of bias, standard setting, and ongoing work for the Department of Defense on establishing gender-neutral entry standards for physically demanding occupations.[5]

Our recommendations are also informed by the vast literature of applied and scientific research that has been conducted on topics such as the validity of tests in employment contexts, successful approaches to increasing diversity, recruiting best-practices, and firefighter selection practices. There are many comprehensive reviews of research in personnel selection (for just a few examples, see Schmidt and Hunter, 1998; Hough and Oswald, 2000; Campion, 1983; Schmitt and Chan, 1998; Salgado, Viswesvaran, and Ones, 2001; Triandis, Kurowski, and Gelfand, 1994).

We also rely on a well-established set of professional practice guidelines in the field of personnel selection to inform our recommendations. These professional practice guidelines are viewed as the authoritative source on the proper development and use of tests and measures in employment contexts. An overview of these guidelines can be found in two published resources:

- *Principles for the Validation and Use of Personnel Selection Procedures* (Society for Industrial and Organizational Psychology, Inc., 2003). This source (referred to as the *Principles*) was produced by the Society for Industrial and Organizational Psychology to "specify established scientific findings and generally accepted professional practice in the field of personnel selection psychology in the choice, development, evaluation, and use of personnel selection procedures designed to measure constructs related to work behavior with a focus on the accuracy of the inferences that underlie employment decisions" (p. 1).

---

[5]   For examples of the past work of some of our authors see: Lim et al., 2009; Lim, Haddad, and Daugherty, 2013; Matthies, Lim, and Keller, 2012; Marquis et al., 2007; Haddad et al., 2012; Hardison et al., 2009; Burkhauser, Hanser, and Hardison, 2014; Manacapilli et al., 2012; Hardison, Sims, and Wong, 2010; Hardison and Vilamovska, 2009; Hardison, 2007; Cullen, Hardison, and Sackett, 2004; Sackett, Hardison, and Cullen, 2004; Hardison and Sackett, 2007; Sims et al., 2014).

- *Standards for Educational and Psychological Testing* (American Educational Research Association et al., 2014). This source (referred to as the *Standards*) was developed jointly by the American Educational Research Association, the American Psychological Association, and the National Council on Measurement in Education. It summarizes professional standards for the development and use of tests in educational, psychological, and employment settings.

This report examines the firefighting selection practices the city currently uses and the existing evidence amassed by the city to support their use. We rely on our past work in these areas, our knowledge of existing work in these areas, and professional practice guidelines to evaluate and recommend changes to the selection practices. We note that research derived from other, albeit similar, selection contexts cannot wholly serve as a substitute for research on the tools used by the city. As such, we also make recommendations for undertaking further data collection to establish validation evidence to support the selection practices. As already stated, the time frame of the study prohibited this additional undertaking.

Although we relied on existing general expertise and knowledge on personnel selection to inform many of our recommendations, we tailored the recommendations specifically to the city's selection processes and selection needs. We therefore reviewed the city's existing processes very closely. In our review we sought to identify not only the issues that the city viewed as its biggest challenges in the selection process, but also the city's goals for improving the selection process. We also carefully reviewed their existing selection processes and supporting materials and met with city personnel to fill in any gaps in the materials the city provided. We supplemented those materials by conducting a quick analysis of disparate impact of the selection process and by interviewing firefighters as a check of the existing job analysis information. The methods for both of these additional efforts are described in the following sections.

Exploratory Interviews to Understand Stakeholder Perspectives

To better understand stakeholders' views on the key goals for the firefighter selection process, we conducted exploratory interviews with key stakeholders listed in Table 1.1.[6] These interviews were largely unstructured and intended to confirm the relevance of the objectives we outlined for the project.

Table 1.1
Stakeholder Interviewees

Fire Chief
Chief Deputy, Administrative Operations
Deputy Chief, Training and Support Bureau
Assistant Chief, Special Operations
Assistant Chief, Employee Relations Division
Deputy Chief, Training and Support
Deputy Chief, Emergency Operations
Fire Inspector
Battalion Chief, Recruit Services Section
Battalion Chief, North Division, Battalion 9, Shift A
Battalion Chief, South Division, Battalion 13, Shift C
Captain II, Station 33
President, Los Angeles Fireman's Relief Association
Head (Captain I), Recruitment Unit
Captain II, Station 94
Captain II, Station 100
Captain II, Station 71
President, LAFD Fire Commission
Vice President, LAFD Fire Commission
LAFD Fire Commissioner
President, United Firefighters of Los Angeles
President, Stentorians
President, Los Bomberos
President, Los Angeles Women in the Fire Service
President, Chief Officers Association
Captain II, Recruitment Unit

---

[6]   All participants in the stakeholder interviews were asked if they would like us to keep their participation confidential or if we could mention them by name in our reports. All agreed to be mentioned by name.

Review of Existing Documentation and Informational Interviews on Recruiting and Selection Processes

To gain a better understanding of the current firefighter selection process, we reviewed existing documentation on the process provided by the Personnel Department. We also met with Personnel Department staff to clarify facts about the selection process and to determine the professional, legal, and financial rationale behind each step in the selection process. A summary of that selection process is provided in Chapter Three.

We also met with members of the LAFD's Recruit Services Section to learn more about the firefighter recruitment and outreach efforts. A summary of the recruiting services role is provided in Chapter Two along with a summary of comments that stakeholders made about possible improvements to the recruiting process.

Job Incumbent Focus Groups to Confirm and Identify New Key Duties, Knowledge, Skills, Abilities, and Other Characteristics for Firefighter Service

We examined three key sources of information in order to document and assess the inherent duties and KSAOs needed to successfully perform the job of firefighter in a large, urban city such as Los Angeles. First, we reviewed a broad range of literature on firefighter job requirements, including online firefighter job descriptions from a variety of fire departments nationwide and the Occupational Information Network (O*NET), an online resource provided by the U.S. Department of Labor Employment and Training Administration.[7] Second, we reviewed an unpublished 1994 job analysis study conducted by the Los Angeles Personnel Department's Research Section and a related 2010 update, also unpublished, that was conducted by a private-sector firm. Finally, we conducted focus group interviews to confirm and supplement the KSAOs identified in 1994 and 2010.

---

[7]   O*NET provides a database that contains information on hundreds of standardized and occupation-specific descriptors. The database is continually updated by surveying a broad range of workers from each occupation.

Data Analyses to Examine Disparate Impact of the 2013 Selection Process

We analyzed quantitative data on the 2013 firefighter applicants (provided by the Personnel Department and the external organization that administers the CPAT) to better understand the impact of the selection process on the race and gender diversity of the firefighter applicants and selectees. The results of the disparate impact analyses are described in Chapter Four.

Organization of This Report

In the next chapter, we present our examination of firefighter recruitment and outreach strategies. In Chapter Three, we provide an overview of the city's firefighter selection process (as it existed at the start of this study), and in Chapter Four we present our statistical analysis of how the selection process was applied to the 2013 cohort of applicants, with a focus on how each step of the process affected the demographic diversity of the applicant pool. We present our recommendations for improving the firefighter selection process in Chapter Five.

We have also included five appendixes that provide further background information and data to support our recommendations. Appendix A provides an overview of key considerations that organizations should have when evaluating a selection process, including validity, reliability, legal defensibility, the value of diversity, and costs. Appendix B summarizes our analysis of key firefighter duties and KSAOs. Appendix C supplements a specific recommendation in Chapter Five—that the LAFD's written test for candidates be sourced to an outside vendor—by providing information on three possible vendors. Finally, Appendixes D and E provide additional technical background on Chapter Five's discussion of the use of random sampling as a possible method for reducing the applicant pool to a manageable size.

CHAPTER TWO

Firefighter Recruitment and Outreach Strategies

Recruiting is a key element in fostering diversity in any organization. Proactive efforts to reach out to the community and generate interest in working for the LAFD, in addition to mentoring future candidates, are among the most effective means of improving the demographic diversity of the candidate pool entering into the selection process. In this chapter, we present a model for applying these issues to the recruiting context. We then summarize the firefighter recruiting process as it existed at the start of our study, based on our informational interviews and reviews of existing documentation.

A Framework for Understanding Recruitment

Figure 2.1 summarizes the range of factors that may affect the quantity and variety of individuals considering a career as a firefighter. The factors fall into two categories. The first consists of the factors that the LAFD can directly leverage to maximize the number and diversity of recruits, such as the LAFD's firefighter recruiting resources and its management of them. The second category consists of a variety of other factors that influence a job seeker's propensity to join the LAFD. For example, propensity can be influenced by the community's views and opinions of the LAFD, individual tastes toward the firefighter profession, and demographic trends and local labor market conditions. While some environmental factors are beyond the direct control of the LAFD, the department can influence propensity to join the LAFD through

Figure 2.1
Factors Influencing the Number and Diversity of LAFD Firefighter Recruits

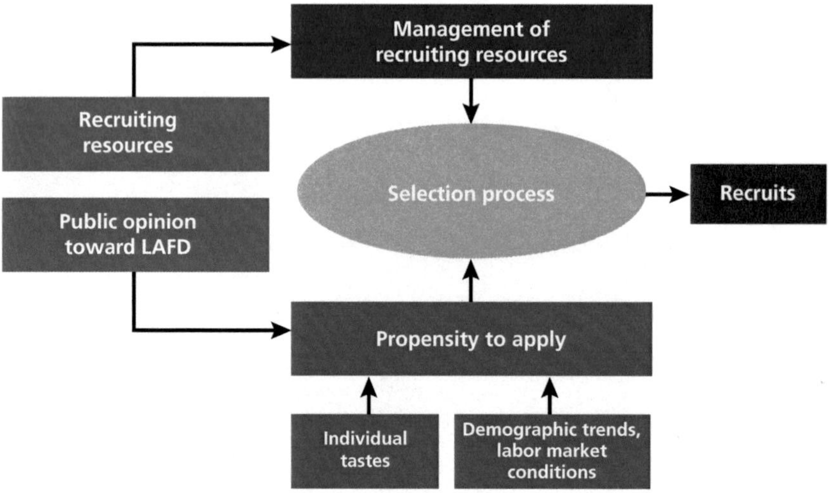

SOURCES: Adapted from Asch and Orvis (1994); Ridgeway et al. (2008); Lim et al. (2009).
RAND *RR687-2.1*

outreach and recruiting resources (Lim et al., 2009). The LAFD can also take steps to influence public opinion.

As shown in the figure, all these factors feed into the selection process: the department's screening and hiring standards, the procedures that applicants must follow during the process, and tests that applicants must take to become a firefighter. The firefighter selection process is detailed in Chapter Three.

Firefighter Recruiting Practices[1]

Officially, outreach and recruitment fall within the purview of the Recruitment Unit—a subset of the LAFD's Recruit Services Section. The Recruitment Unit's budget (provided by the Personnel Depart-

---

[1]   Note that this summary pertains to the recruiting practices in existence at the time of this study.

ment, not the LAFD) for outreach and recruitment activities is approximately $105,000 per year.[2] Approximately six LAFD personnel make up the broader Recruit Services Section, which is headed by a battalion chief and primarily focuses on operational and administrative issues related to the firefighter training program and selection process. The Recruitment Unit is headed by a captain first class and staffed by three individuals: a captain first class, a captain second class, and a civilian clerk. Their outreach and recruitment responsibilities entail attending job fairs, conducting school visitations, and attending community events. Recruiting through these three types of events has been an LAFD mainstay through several hiring cycles. The Recruitment Unit introduces interested individuals to the fire service at these events and encourages them to visit the firefighter recruitment website for more information on applying and selection. The city has developed a recruitment tracking system to help the LAFD track the success of outreach events. But we do not know whether this tracking system has resulted in increased website visitations and submitted applications.

Many outreach and recruitment efforts have been undertaken by individual firefighters, fire captains, and battalion chiefs volunteering their off-duty and vacation hours. This pattern has persisted over the past few hiring cycles. Though in general they were not paid for their time, some were offered a special compensation pay called "V-time" in exchange for their help with mentoring and recruitment. V-time still exists and is currently administered in the same capacity, but some interviewees stated that compensation pay is a poor incentive for firefighters to work on their off days. Interviewees felt that because mentoring and preparatory training is a painstaking process, asking firefighters to partition their already-limited time may not be a sustainable solution. Yet, many still find time to help with outreach. For example, efforts such as the youth fire academies and the LAFD Cadet Program are community-based and focus on individuals who may be interested in the fire service but have yet to apply. There are four youth fire academies in the greater Los Angeles area. Although they instruct partici-

---

[2] The Personnel Department's involvement—such as maintaining the website, ordering supplies, arranging media campaigns, etc.—is not included in this amount.

pants on the ins-and-outs of firefighting in particular, they generally focus on equipping youth with life skills and professional guidance. They often serve as precursors to the Cadet Program, which many youth join after graduating from a fire academy. Compared to the youth fire academies, the Cadet Program is more specialized and functions as an internship that introduces youth to the culture and expectations of the LAFD. Both initiatives are organized and managed by various fire captains and battalion chiefs.

Categorically, the youth fire academies and Cadet Program are considered outreach and recruitment efforts and both have good minority participation. However, very few cadets and youth fire academy graduates become firefighters. One could argue that people who volunteer for or apply to these programs are already sold on the merits of a career in the LAFD. Thus a starker challenge is finding ways to use the programs to reach highly qualified minority groups that will actually apply to the LAFD and be competitive. This could mean using the programs to help stir up interest in minority groups that might otherwise have regarded the job of firefighter as unattainable or undesirable, or have not considered it at all. In other words, these programs could be specifically designed to help generate interest in otherwise disinterested groups.

Key Comments on Recruiting from the Interviews

Our interviews with stakeholders were largely exploratory and intended to give us a sense of what they perceived as being the primary issues concerning the current selection process. The questions we asked varied depending on the person's role and his or her relationship to the LAFD. Our questions evolved and changed as we learned more about the selection process. As a result, applying a systematic process of counting or coding the results of these discussions might be misleading. We therefore refrained from providing specific counts or estimates of how many people agreed with a given comment. Instead we made note of comments that pertained to recruiting to show that some of our participants believe improved recruiting efforts are part of the solution.

For example, with respect to improving current recruiting practices, our participants reported that a lack of sufficient funds and available personnel significantly impacts the time, resources, and effort invested in firefighter outreach and recruitment. Some of our interview participants also stated that expanding the recruiting budget and staff would favorably impact outreach and recruiting efforts across the city.[3] Additionally, some commented that an obvious tool for recruiting— particularly in this age of smart phones and widespread Internet access—is the current LAFD website and the use of social media. The website currently includes a number of informational elements directed at generating interest in firefighter jobs, descriptions of the highly competitive nature of the screening process, and links to Twitter and Facebook. However, the website could certainly be enriched. Enhancing the website and using social media are two areas in recruiting and outreach that could be accomplished with minimal costs.

Some of our interviewees reported a belief that some members of minority groups and women especially, have had a lower propensity to apply for firefighter positions compared with white males, especially given recent negative media coverage of the firefighter hiring process. Overall, the stakeholders we interviewed generally believed that improving the diversity of the applicant pool is possible with a long-term outreach and recruitment campaign.

The Emphasis Should Be on Finding Highly Qualified Candidates, Not Merely on Increasing the Quantity of Candidates

One goal of outreach and recruiting efforts is to increase the number of women and racial minorities who apply to the LAFD. However, as we show in the next chapter, the number of applicants who enter the selection process already dwarfs the number of available positions each

---

[3]   Although some might assume that recruiter race could be important in attracting more minorities, research suggests that other recruiter characteristics (including personableness and the consistent and fair treatment of people being recruited) matter more than race or gender (Chapman et al., 2005).

year. As we discuss in Chapter Five, we recommend that the LAFD and the Personnel Department implement a mechanism for reducing the number of applicants to a manageable size and discuss two distinct options for doing so.

Given the large number of total applications, merely increasing the number of minority applicants cannot be the sole focus of recruiting. In fact, it appears that the city is doing a fairly good job of attracting minority applicants. For example, Figures 2.2 and 2.3 show that current recruiting efforts have attracted an overrepresentation of black and Native American applicants, when compared with the broader Los

Figure 2.2
Los Angeles County Population (Census Data)

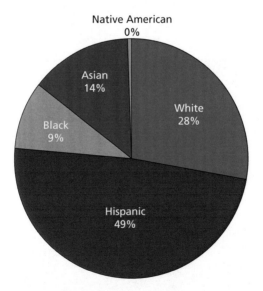

SOURCE: U.S. Census Bureau (2010).
RAND RR687-2.2

Figure 2.3
Firefighter Applicants Meeting Minimum Requirements

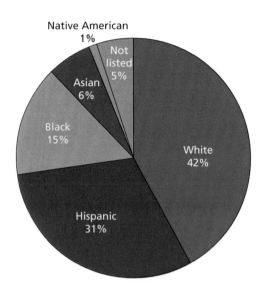

SOURCE: Personnel Department 2013 applicant cohort data.
RAND *RR687-2.3*

Angeles County population,[4] suggesting that current efforts are effective in generating interest within these minority groups. Yet, we also see in the next chapter that racial minority (and female) applicants are not as competitive at the early stages of the selection process as white (and male) applicants. Thus, a key goal should be to identify and recruit highly qualified racial minority and female applicants without overburdening the system with large numbers of applicants of any race or gender who are unlikely to be competitive. Meeting this challenge

---

[4]   Note that we include Los Angeles County census data here for a quick illustration of the overrepresentation of minorities in the applicant pool only. However, LAFD applicants come from all over. It would therefore probably be more accurate to include the other four surrounding counties: San Bernardino, Riverside, Ventura, and Orange. Also, the relevant qualified labor force (those who are employable) is different than the general population. For these reasons, a better comparison group might be one that included other populations from nearby counties and that was restricted to only those meeting at least the minimum entry qualifications.

could result in greater perceptions of fairness if it led to significant improvements in the proportion of highly qualified minority applicants who are ultimately hired.

CHAPTER THREE

The 2013 Firefighter Selection Process

The firefighter selection process (as it was applied in 2013 and as it existed at the start of this study) is described below. Our description of the process is based on several interviews we conducted with the Personnel Department to understand the process as it existed at the time the interviews were conducted.[1]

The 2013 firefighter selection process consisted of ten steps, with participation from the Fire Department, the Personnel Department, and an external organization that administered the CPAT, the California Fire Fighter Joint Apprentice Committee. It took about a year for a candidate to move through the entire process (Figure 3.1).

We describe each step of the 2013 process, including the purpose and content of each step, who administered it, where the step occurred, and when it occurred. (Recommendations regarding changes to each step are discussed in Chapter Five.) Although there was no clearly specified waiting period between each step, we report the timeline for the latest test administration. Where available, we also provide information as to passing minimums, the approximate numbers of candidates entering and passing, and the cost of each step. Also, where available, we provide information relayed by the Personnel Department on policy guidance and restrictions.

---

[1]   Note, however, that the city instituted a different process just prior to completion of our study, well after our interviews were complete. As a result, the summary below does not reflect those changes.

Figure 3.1
Timeline of 2013 Firefighter Selection Process

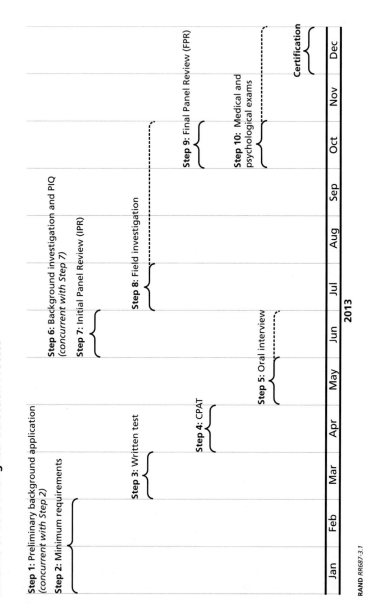

Notification Cards

Interested candidates could file notification cards with the Personnel Department to be alerted when a new job bulletin was posted. Between July 2009 and July 2012, about 26,000 people filed notification cards. The Personnel Department asked candidates to re-file in July 2012 if they were still interested, and about 12,000 did so.

Step 1: Preliminary Background Application

In the first step, starting in January 2013 for the most recent cycle, applicants completed the preliminary background application. This was an online form with basic background questions about applicants' employment history, financial history, drug history, and additional topics such as whether applicants have car insurance. The firefighter recruitment website lists factors, such as a history of drug use, that could make applicants less competitive than other applicants and, in some cases, unlikely to succeed through the process.

Step 2: Describing the Minimum Requirements

Although we do not consider meeting a set of minimum requirements to be a step in its own right, the city's outline of Personnel Department processes considered it as such. The requirements were as follows:

- Candidates must be at least 18 years old and have graduated from high school or have an equivalent credential.
- Candidates must pass the CPAT.
- Candidates must obtain a valid emergency medical technician (EMT) certificate.
- Candidates must have a valid California driver's license.

Candidates were informed of these requirements by the job posting at the beginning of each cycle. This step therefore happened concurrently with Step 1, in January, although candidates were informed that they had until the final stage of the selection process to obtain EMT certification and a valid California driver's license.

Step 3: Written Test

Test of Reading Comprehension, Arithmetic, and Mechanical Aptitude

The written test was a 100-item multiple-choice exam covering three content areas: reading comprehension (approximately 40 questions), arithmetic (approximately 40 questions), and mechanical aptitude (approximately 20 questions). The Personnel Department adjusted the test's minimum passing score to the highest score that also minimized the disparate impact on the demographic diversity of the applicant pool.[2] As a result, the minimum varied by year, depending on the candidate pool's performance. For the 2013 hiring cycle, the Personnel Department set the minimum passing score at 70 percent.

In 2013, the Personnel Department administered the test on March 2 and 3 in the Los Angeles Convention Center (at no cost to the applicants). Although more than 13,000 applicants were scheduled for a written test, roughly 4,000 did not show up to take it. Of the 9,600 or so candidates who took the test, about 6,500 passed.

The Personnel Department hired more than 100 proctors and supplemented them with its own staff to meet the demand. The cost of the convention center was roughly $20,000 and the proctors roughly $6,000. This does not include the cost of the full-time staff or the cost to score the test, among other expenses.

---

[2]   This is accomplished by examining disparate impact ratios for each minority group and picking a minimum test score that tends to improve those ratios. Disparate impact ratios are explained in Chapter Four. Professional guidelines such as the *Standards* and *Principles* suggest setting test score minimums in a way that links the score to minimum acceptable levels of performance on the job. This particular method for setting test score minimums does not do that.

Test Development

The written test was developed by the Personnel Department using a preparatory process that spanned from July to December 2012. The selection process was developed in consultation with a yearlong working committee that included the Personnel Department employees, the United Firefighters of Los Angeles City, and various members of LAFD employee groups. Two separate job analyses (studies describing the results of a systematic process for defining important or frequent job tasks—one from 2010 and one from 1994) and a 1996 criterion validation study (conducted using LAFD data) were also consulted and used to guide the test content (all are unpublished).[3]

A section on mechanical aptitude was added in 1994, then removed when the 1996 criterion-related validation study did not find a significant correlation between candidates' prior mechanical aptitude test and job success. The mechanical aptitude section was added back in the 2013 process to address a recommendation in the LAFD's most recent job analysis.

Test questions were selected from the Personnel Department's internal item bank system and a vendor item bank (the Western Region Item Bank) to address reading comprehension, mathematics, and mechanical aptitude. The Personnel Department's internal item bank questions are collected from all tests ever given and were developed by subject-matter experts and other analysts from the Personnel Department. Questions were not specific to firefighting and therefore could be used on any civil service exam. However, items were considered for inclusion on the firefighter exam only if they appeared to relate in some way to situations that firefighters might face. Each year, new questions were chosen by Personnel Department staff.

---

3   We reviewed these unpublished studies and discussed the test content development with the Personnel Department. Although those originally responsible for the creation of the test may have sought to link the reports to the test content, to our knowledge, the process used to do so was not formally documented anywhere. Therefore, we strongly suggest that new efforts be undertaken to do so now and formally document the results.

Step 4: Candidate Physical Ability Test

The Personnel Department used to have its own in-house physical ability test, but the LAFD argued that it was not sufficiently rigorous or closely related to firefighting. That test was developed by research psychologists and consisted of exercises such as side steps, step tests, and leg lifts. The CPAT was adopted because it is used by a number of fire departments across the country and the Personnel Department reports that it is legally defensible.[4] Although fewer women are able to pass the CPAT than men, they do pass the CPAT at higher rates than many other physical tests (Hulett et al., 2007). In addition, because participating in a training program can significantly improve candidates' chances of passing the CPAT,[5] the LAFD website directed applicants interested in training to a free resource that discusses how to train for the CPAT.[6]

Candidates had to submit valid proof that they had passed the CPAT to move on to the next step. After candidates were informed that they had passed the written test, they had five days to submit their CPAT certification.

The volume of demand was unexpectedly large for the 2013 applicant cohort. The official starting time for accepting CPAT certifications was 8:00 a.m. on April 22, 2013. Most candidates submitted their CPAT certifications by email on that day, but many others sent them in by fax or waited in line overnight. Of the candidates who submitted CPAT certifications on April 22, about one-third (around 965 people) submitted them in the first minute at 8:00 a.m.. Because the Personnel Department had established a policy of processing people

---

[4]   In 2006, the International Association of Firefighters signed a conciliation agreement with the U.S. Equal Employment Opportunity Commission that makes it unlikely that any legal challenge to the CPAT would be successful (International Association of Fire Chiefs, 2009).

[5]   Hulett et al. (2007) finds that across all tests, departments that train their firefighters before physical testing report a pass rate of women of 52.6 percent, compared to the pass rate of 34.6 percent reported by departments without training.

[6]   The LAFD website included a link to California Fire Fighter Joint Apprenticeship Committee, 2007.

in the order in which their test results were received, and because far more candidates submitted CPAT certifications than could be interviewed, only those 965 or so who submitted their certifications in that first minute at 8:00 a.m. were allowed to continue on in the process. Accordingly, anyone who did not submit their CPAT certification in the first minute was not selected for an interview.[7]

Step 5: Oral Interview

Job Interview with a Firefighter and Interview Specialist

In 2013, the oral interview was the only face-to-face interaction candidates had with the LAFD. The interviews were held from May 13 through June 25. The interviews, which lasted from 20 minutes to 45 minutes each, were run by a fire captain and an interview specialist. The interview specialists—typically retired city workers with experience in human resources—were hired temporarily by the Personnel Department to conduct the firefighter hiring interviews. The fire captain was a volunteer from the LAFD. The interviewers were required to sign a confidentiality form and confirm that they did not know any of the candidates and thus had no conflict of interest in that role.

The Personnel Department trained the LAFD interviewers and the interview specialists using written materials and a video. The training emphasized the importance of evaluating a candidate's past performance rather than the interviewer's gut impressions of them.

Interview questions were developed by the Personnel Department in 2004 to cover the core competencies of the firefighting position, defined as follows:

- Job motivation
- Initiative in learning
- Practical orientation
- Adaptability

---

[7] As noted in Chapter One, according to media accounts, this "first come, first served" approach was viewed as unfair by many applicants.

- Service orientation
- Teamwork
- Respect for others
- Oral communication.

Interviewers were free to choose from a list of questions, but they were required to ask at least one question about each rating factor.

All interviewers were trained to use an interview worksheet to rate candidates on each of the eight competencies and assign an overall score. The interview worksheet detailed each competency along with descriptive benchmarks. For each competency, there were four ratings and their corresponding scores, which ranged from 65 to 105.[8] The ratings were "unfavorable evidence" (score of 65), "minimal favorable evidence" (70–79), "favorable evidence" (80–89), and "very favorable evidence" (90–100). Examples were provided to guide the interviewer's judgment. Unfavorable evidence for job motivation, for example, included, "Views position as 'just a job'" or "Unable to relate applicability of experience to position." Very favorable evidence included, "Broad expectations/understanding of accomplishment in position" and "Experience beneficial to performance of duties/responsibilities." The interviewers were trained to support the scores they assigned by taking notes throughout the interview worksheet, but there was no formal calculation or checklist. Once each interviewer had filled out their answers for each competency, they assigned an overall score. The interviewers first came up with scores independently from one another. They then discussed their scores and came to a consensus.

While 70 was considered a passing score, candidates had to earn one of the top three scores—95, 100, or 105—to progress to the next step. This "rule of three whole scores" is in place throughout the civil service examination system and is defined in the City of Los Angeles Charter and Civil Service Rules (see Appendix A). If too few candidates score 95 or above, the Personnel Department can add lower-

---

[8]   Scores can go as high as 105 if the candidate has military experience: As discussed in Appendix A, there is a 5 percent bonus for such experience.

scoring candidates to the accepted pool until the number of candidates is equal to the number of vacancies plus five.

For the 2013 applicant cohort, about 600 of the 900 or so candidates interviewed scored 95 or above. Interview specialist costs were roughly $6,000 in 2013; the cost of LAFD staff was not available.

Step 6: Background Investigation and Preliminary Investigative Questionnaire

Collection of Preliminary Background Information Using Applicant-Provided Information

After candidates completed the interview, they were scheduled for a preliminary background check, which proceeded in two parts. The candidates were first asked to fill out the Personal History Form (PHF) and bring back supporting documentation within roughly two weeks. The personal history form was similar to that given to other public safety positions, although it was less in-depth than that of potential police officers. Because firefighters are not considered sworn peace officers (like police officers are), the same laws that restrict what may be asked of civilians are in effect for firefighters as well. Candidates were asked to list their residences for the past ten years, name their family members, describe their past experience and employment, and other basic questions. The PHF also asked if they had ever been in auto accidents or convicted of a felony or misdemeanor and asked them to describe the current state of their finances. Candidates had to give seven personal references and bring in supporting documentation (Social Security card, proof of auto insurance, EMT license, etc.).

Candidates were then invited to a classroom setting, where they filled out an in-depth Preliminary Investigative Questionnaire (PIQ) asking them a variety of questions on their personal history, such as their personal conduct and any activities violating the law, military history, firefighter and law enforcement applications and experience, finances, vehicle operation, residence, employment, alcohol consumption, narcotic and substance abuse, and questions regarding negative, undesirable, and unlawful behaviors. For example, candidates were asked whether they had ever been involved in or been associated with anyone involved in acts of forgery or prostitution, whether anyone had ever complained about their work performance, or whether any family members were associated with gangs. Candidates filled out this form and then sat with an investigator for 40 minutes to go over their answers. Any illegal or otherwise concerning activities had to be explained in detail, but there were no disqualifying answers.

The investigator then made a recommendation in the candidate's file about whether or not the candidate should proceed in the process. This recommendation, however, was not deterministic. The candidate automatically moved on to the next step, regardless of the investigator's recommendation.

This cycle's background investigations were held in June 2013. Expenses for background investigations during 2013 added up to roughly $286,000, including hiring background investigators, interview specialists, case managers, and clerical support.

Step 7: Initial Panel Review

Two Fire Captains Review the Candidate's Initial Background Application Package

The findings in the PIQ, along with the personal history form and the interview worksheet, were given to a panel for review.[9] The panel consisted of two fire captain volunteers, but the LAFD ultimately decided who would sit on the panel. It looked for diversity, sought out captains unrelated to the candidates, and asked the potential panel members to fairly evaluate all of the applicants, but there were no other explicitly stated requirements for who could serve. The Personnel Department did not have a representative on the panel, but it did train the panel in how to conduct the review and what to look for.

The primary stated objectives of both the background and field investigations (Step 8 in the selection process) were to identify past, and

---

[9]   Note that these panel members are not those who participated in the job interview or the background interview.

especially recent, behaviors that illustrate the types of actions desired and not desired of LAFD candidates. The background investigation process was intended to tap behaviors relevant to six background standards developed by the Personnel Department in 2012, under the authority of the city's Civil Service Commission, to be the standards considered essential for success in public safety firefighter employment. The following are the six background standards:

- Interpersonal skills, sensitivity, and respect for others
- Decisionmaking and judgment
- Maturity and discipline
- Honesty, integrity, and personal ethics
- Setting and achieving goals
- Record checks.

Panel reviewers were given the background standards for public safety positions. They were also shown a PowerPoint presentation discussing confidentiality and describing the rating factors. Finally, they went through example packets and discussed as a group their thoughts on whether example candidates met the background standards. This training lasts at least a half day.

All panel reviewers were trained to use a detailed rating form to assign overall ratings of "Outstanding," "Good," "Satisfactory," and "Unsatisfactory" for each candidate. For each of the six background standards listed above, the rating sheet provided examples of behavior (anchors) to help reviewers judge a candidate's suitability and asked reviewers to provide brief but specific comments about the candidate's fitness on each standard. One criterion for the "maturity and discipline" background standard, for example, was that the reviewer had to choose between the words "no," "slight," "some," and "significant" to fill in the blank in the following sentence:

[BLANK] indications of being argumentative, defensive, or blaming others (or circumstances) for mistakes made.

Reviewers were trained to give candidates ratings on each standard and then to decide independently on a final overall rating. Reviewers did not have to reach consensus about the overall rating, but the ratings were supposed to be within one rating level of one another. For example, if one reviewer rated a candidate "Good," the second rating had to be either "Good," "Outstanding," or "Satisfactory" (only one step away from "Good"). A pair of ratings such as "Good" and "Unsatisfactory" (two steps apart) was not acceptable. In cases where their independent rating was two or more steps apart, the reviewers were trained to discuss the difference and, if possible, adjust their scores based on the discussion. Candidates had to be rated at least "Good" by both reviewers to pass.[10]

Reviews took place during June 2013, concurrent with background investigations. For the 2013 applicant cohort, only candidates receiving a rating of "Outstanding" by both reviewers moved on in the process, although eventually a small number of additional candidates were allowed to progress with slightly lower ratings.

Step 8: Field Investigation

In-Depth Background Check

Candidates who passed the Initial Panel Review then underwent a thorough background check. In this step, experienced investigators (including some retired police officers) were hired as members of the Personnel Department's background investigations staff to check candidates' records and references thoroughly.

Investigators collected a range of information to determine whether a candidate met the six background standards listed. They combined information from the PHF, PIQ, fingerprint analysis, Department of Motor Vehicles records, and TransUnion reports. They also reviewed and interviewed references and knocked on the doors of friends, neighbors, etc., to corroborate the information the candidate had furnished. An investigation could last from 30 to 180 days depending on the com-

---

[10] This meant that a single rater could prevent a candidate from moving on. Because there may be rater error operating in such cases, the Personnel Department should consider establishing procedures to address this (e.g., by adding a third rater in cases where there are discrepancies, if this process is continued.

plexity of the investigation. Background investigators summarized the information they found and made recommendations about suitability on the final forms submitted for the Final Panel Review, but they did not have the ability to disqualify candidates.

Step 9: Final Panel Review

Repeat of Initial Panel Review with Corroborated Information

In the Final Panel Review, an LAFD captain and battalion chief repeated the process of the Initial Panel Review. Reviewers examined a packet of information about the candidate, which included the corroborated information the field investigator found. They filled out the same forms as Initial Panel Review, adding to the Initial Panel Review's comments. Again, a rating of "Good" from both reviewers was required to pass, but only candidates who were rated "Outstanding" moved on.

The Personnel Department provided training to the reviewers, similar to what is provided for the initial panel reviewers. In the past, the Personnel Department was more involved, but its recent role was limited to training reviewers and checking that documentation was properly completed and all ratings were supported.

Step 10: Medical and Psychological Evaluations

The physical exam established the candidate's physical condition, including vital signs, height and weight, eye and hearing tests, metabolic blood workups, organ system evaluation, urinalysis, pulmonary function, treadmill test, and a few other simple evaluations.

The psychological exam included the Minnesota Multiphasic Personality Inventory (MMPI)[11] and a questionnaire created by the city's Medical Services Division. Psychologists sent the MMPI out to be scored. Based on those results and the information in the background

---

[11] The MMPI is a psychological test commonly used by mental health professionals to assess and diagnose mental illness. It was developed in the 1930s by psychologists at the University of Minnesota and remains one of the most frequently used clinical testing instruments.

investigation, reviewers chose whether to pass a candidate, fail them, or bring them in for an interview.

The Personnel Department and LAFD were not told why a candidate failed on medical or psychological grounds per the Health Insurance Portability and Accountability Act (HIPAA) and Americans with Disabilities Act guidelines, although a candidate could ask for that information in writing.

Candidates at this step could also be deferred for these two exams (rather than failed); hence, not all candidates made it through this screening step in time to be considered for the current training cycle. Deferment could be granted for cases where the applicant could correct a health problem (e.g., have surgery to address a vision impairment, lose weight). In addition, the process could also take a long time as some candidates were required to collect various medical charts or complete a variety of psychological interviews and medical exam appointments,[12] which could in turn lead to follow-up tests and documentation. For these reasons, some candidates who passed this step might not have passed in time to be placed on the final certification list.

Certification

After candidates passed all the necessary medical and psychological tests, they were put on the certification list indicating that they were certified for firefighter hiring consideration by LAFD if a training slot were available.[13]

---

[12] As noted above, in addition to filling out standardized forms and completing the aforementioned psychological tests, some applicants were required to complete interviews with the medical and psychological staff as part of the screening process.

[13] Note that the certification list is only valid for a finite period of time.

CHAPTER FOUR

Statistical Analysis of the Selection Process

In this chapter, we report findings from our statistical analysis of the firefighter selection process, using the 2013 cohort of applicants. The objective of this analysis was twofold: (1) to identify steps in the process where a large proportion of the applicants were eliminated and (2) to identify steps in the process that affected the racial, ethnic, and gender representation of the applicant pool. The former can assist in identifying the steps most useful for narrowing the applicant pool, and the latter can inform which elements in the process are most likely to affect diversity. We considered these findings in formulating our recommendations to improve efficiency, minimize potential disparate impact on diversity, and improve the overall fairness and transparency of the firefighter hiring process.

Data

We obtained data from the Personnel Department on all firefighter candidates screened in the 2013 hiring process. Before analyzing the selection process, we reviewed the applicant data files for discrepancies and duplicate information. In a small number of cases, we eliminated applicant records because they appeared in the file more than once, and we adjusted applicant records that were implausible (e.g., when there was evidence of not passing an early step followed by evidence of passing all subsequent steps). Therefore, our numbers approximate but are not identical to those published by the Personnel Department. The full selection process includes a number of intermediary steps—including filling out paperwork, scheduling, and showing up in person—that are part of the ten steps outlined by the Personnel Department (as described in the previous chapter). However, for the results presented in this chapter, we are concerned only with those steps that involve an explicit decision point (i.e., continue on in the process or reject). As such, in this chapter, some intermediary steps are combined and reported as a single decision point.

We also obtained summary statistics on CPAT pass rates from the CPAT testing office in Orange County, California, to estimate what the pass rates would have looked like for the CPAT step had the pass rates not been restricted by the "first come, first served" approach for narrowing the applicant pool.

Reduction of Applicants in the Selection Process

Table 4.1 documents movement through the process for the 2013 applicant cohort, showing the total number of applicants at each stage and the proportion passing from the previous step, by ethnicity and gender of the applicants. A total of 13,236 applicants began the process (at Steps 1 and 2), with 187 making it through each of the ten steps. For the final step of the process—"passed medical and psychological evaluations"—we consider applicants having passed if they passed *or were deferred* for both exams. Deferment can be granted for cases where the applicant can receive treatment to correct a health problem as discussed in the previous chapter.

The first step in the process is to apply and to meet the minimum requirements of being at least 18 years of age and having a high school diploma or equivalent. For each subsequent step, we calculate the proportion of candidates passing based on the total number of candidates passing the previous step.

To identify steps in the process where the majority of the applicants were eliminated, we present the volume of applicants eliminated per 1,000 applicants in Figure 4.1. We calibrated the proportions to a starting applicant pool of 1,000 for ease of interpretation. The lion's share of applicants meeting the minimum eligibility requirements was

Table 4.1
Number and Percentage Moving on at Each Selection Step, 2013 Applicant Cohort

	All Applicants	White	Hispanic	Black	Asian	Native American	Race Not Listed	Male	Female	Gender Not Listed
Steps 1 and 2: Filled out preliminary background application and met minimum requirements	13,236	5,509	4,160	1,960	869	129	609	12,391	669	176
Step 3: Took and passed written test	6,504 (49%)	3,274 (59%)	1,912 (46%)	389 (20%)	524 (60%)	75 (58%)	330 (54%)	6,133 (49%)	267 (40%)	104 (59%)
Step 4: Submitted CPAT certification within time window	966 (15%)	566 (17%)	251 (13%)	44 (11%)	64 (12%)	10 (13%)	31 (9%)	935 (15%)	21 (8%)	10 (10%)
Step 5: Scheduled and passed oral interview	622 (64%)	371 (66%)	156 (62%)	33 (75%)	47 (73%)	7 (70%)	8 (26%)	602 (64%)	19 (90%)	1 (10%)
Steps 6 and 7: Filled out PIQ and passed Initial Panel Review	446 (72%)	270 (73%)	108 (69%)	19 (58%)	40 (85%)	4 (57%)	5 (63%)	433 (72%)	12 (63%)	1 (100%)
Steps 8 and 9: Passed in-depth background check and Final Panel Review	205 (46%)	121 (45%)	55 (51%)	6 (32%)	19 (48%)	2 (50%)	2 (40%)	202 (47%)	3 (25%)	0 (0%)
Step 10: Passed medical and psychological evaluations	187 (91%)	107 (88%)	52 (95%)	6 (100%)	18 (95%)	2 (100%)	2 (100%)	184 (91%)	3 (100%)	0 (0%)

SOURCE: Los Angeles Personnel Department data on 2013 LAFD firefighter applications.

NOTES: Percentage is calculated as the number of people who passed the hurdle divided by the number who passed the prior hurdle. The two "Not Listed" columns pertain to the 609 applicants who did not report their ethnicity and 176 applicants who did not report their gender.

Figure 4.1
1,000 Hypothetical Applicants Retained and Lost Through Firefighter Evaluation and Investigation Strategies

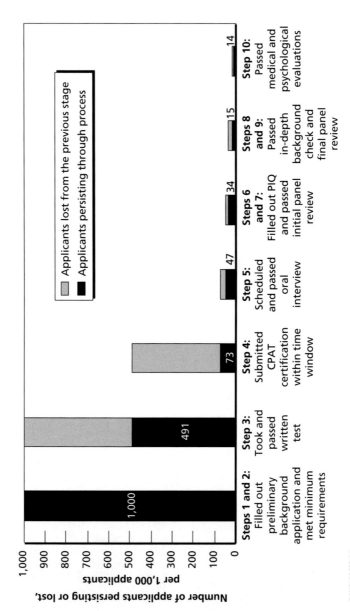

RAND RR687-4.1

eliminated by the written exam (Step 3) and the CPAT certification submission time window (Step 4). For every 1,000 eligible applicants, 491 showed up for and passed the written exam. Conversely, failing to take and pass the written exam eliminated more than half of the applicants. Of the remaining 491 per 1,000, only 73 submitted documentation of passing their CPAT within the time window. There is more of a gradual elimination of applicants across the subsequent six steps, except at Steps 8 and 9, when half of the remaining applicants are eliminated.

In addition to the CPAT data from the Personnel Department, information provided to us by the Orange County CPAT testing center indicates that about 94 percent of the people who take the CPAT pass it. Hence, the CPAT itself does not eliminate many applicants.

The Selection Process's Impact on Minorities

We explored two methods for measuring whether minorities were adversely impacted for each step in the firefighter selection process: the *80% rule* and testing for statistical significance. Both are commonly discussed as relevant in determining whether a selection practice shows evidence of disparate impact.[1] Results for each of these methods are presented in Table 4.2.

Both methods involve comparing the selection ratios of each protected group to the selection ratio of the other groups. In Table 4.2, this is calculated as:

$$(p) \text{ MINORITY}_k \, / \, (p) \text{ MAJORITY}_k$$

where (p) MINORITY$_k$ is the proportion (p) of the minority group (MINORITY) passing step k (where $k = 1...n$) in the hiring pro-

---

[1]   There is no single accepted measure for establishing disparate impact; however, tests of statistical significance and the 80% rule are the two most commonly used measures. Both have pros and cons. Additionally, with respect to statistical significance, no single statistical test is definitively supported as the right test to use. For more discussion on this, see Peresie (2009).

cess, and (p) MAJORITY$_k$ is the proportion (p) of the majority group (MAJORITY) passing the same step in the hiring process.

In the case of the 80% rule (or 4/5ths rule), if the ratio resulting from this formula is less than 0.80, then by some standards (e.g., see the see the Equal Employment Opportunity Commission's [EEOC's] *Uniform Guidelines*, 1978) that selection step is considered to have disparate impact on the minority group.[2] This is discussed in more detail in Appendix A. For example, the proportion of black applicants taking and passing the written test relative to those who filled out the preliminary background application and met minimum requirements was 0.198 (or about 20 percent, as reported in Table 4.1) and the proportion of white applicants was 0.594 (or about 60 percent). The corresponding impact ratio is calculated as 0.198/0.594 = 0.333. This means that black applicants passed this step in the process at about a third of the rate of whites. Because this ratio is less than 0.80, this step in the hiring process would be considered to have disparate impact on black applicants, according to the 80% rule.

Analyses of impact using the 0.80 threshold are prone to Type I errors—that is, they may detect a difference in passing rates that is in fact due to chance rather than a discriminatory selection step. Therefore, as noted above, we also apply a different criterion for exploring whether a step in the process shows disparate impact. We calculate a z-test for statistical differences between the two proportions—(p) MINORITY$_k$ and (p) MAJORITY$_k$—and denote p-values smaller than 0.05 as statistically significant.[3]

---

[2]   Note that while the EEOC and other federal agencies have adopted this rule in disparate impact cases, neither the U.S. Supreme Court nor any Circuit Court of Appeals has adopted it. Those courts have instead used a case-by-case approach for analysis of disparate impact cases.

[3]   Although a significance test comparing two proportions can help determine whether the observed differences appear to be not due to chance alone, this test cannot tell us whether a similar difference should be expected to occur in future applicant pools. If the applicant pools for each race and gender in the 2013 data are, for some reason, not representative of applicant pools that would occur in the future, Type I errors—or incorrectly concluding that there would be disparate impact in the future—could still occur. Type II errors—or incorrectly concluding that there would be no disparate impact in the future—could also occur for the same reasons.

Results of both tests (the test of statistical significance and the 80% rule) are shown in Table 4.2. We shade the cells of those comparisons where the impact ratio is both below 0.80 and the difference in proportions yields a difference that is statistically significant at the 95 percent level.

As mentioned at the outset of this chapter, here we are concerned only with steps that involve an explicit decision point (i.e., continue on in the process or reject). This is why Steps 6 and 7 and Steps 8 and 9 are each combined into a single column in Table 4.2. Steps 6 and 7 involve only one selection decision. People have to both fill out the PIQ and pass the Initial Panel Review in order to receive a selection decision. Moreover, only a small subset of the people who passed the prior interview step failed to fill out the PIQ (of the 622 who passed the interview, 607 showed up to fill out the PIQ). Similarly, Step 3, the written test, involves intermediary steps of (1) taking the test and (2)

Table 4.2. Ethnic and Gender Differences in Rates of Passing Each Step of the Firefighter Evaluation and Investigation Process, 2013 Applicant Cohort

	Step 3: Took and Passed Written Test	Step 4: Submitted CPAT Certification Within Time Window	Step 5: Scheduled and Passed Oral Interview	Steps 6 and 7: Filled Out PIQ and Passed Initial Panel Review	Steps 8 and 9: Passed In-Depth Background Check and Final Panel Review	Step 10: Passed Medical and Psychological Evaluations
Hispanic v. white	0.77*	0.76*	0.95	0.95	1.14	1.07
Black v. white	0.33*	0.65*	1.14	0.79	0.70	1.13
Asian v. white	1.01	0.71*	1.12	1.17*	1.06	1.07
Female v. male	0.81*	0.52*	1.41*	0.88	0.54	1.10

SOURCE: Los Angeles Personnel Department.

NOTES: Ratios lower than the 0.80 threshold and that are statistically different from the comparison group are shown in shaded cells.

* Indicates that the proportion passing is statistically different from the comparison group at $p < 0.05$.

passing the test. Lastly, Step 10 includes two separate tests; however, the order in which passing each test occurs depends on the applicant; hence, it could not be separated out as a separate step. We treated these all as single decision points in Table 4.2, although we did examine the available data on who took the test versus who passed it.

For example, as shown in Table 4.3, many people who were invited to take the written test failed to do so. There were some differences across race groups in rates of who showed up (e.g., black applicants showed up at lower rates than other groups), but the differences did not violate the 80% rule. Instead, most of the impact for Step 3 occurred in terms of how many of the candidates who showed up for the test passed it (e.g., only 22 percent of black applicants who took the test passed, compared with 59 percent of white applicants).[4]

As noted above, we also solicited CPAT information from the Orange County CPAT testing center. According to its data (shown in Table 4.4), the CPAT itself does not violate the 80% rule for minority test takers. It does, however, still violate it for women, although the impact is smaller.

Caution in Interpreting These Estimates Is Warranted

Although Table 4.2 clearly shows that the tools used in the later stages of firefighter selection exhibited less disparate impact for many of the groups than the tools used earlier in the process, it is important to note that such a finding may be misleading. That finding alone cannot rule out the possibility that disparate impact could occur on those later

---

[4] It is not possible for us to separate data in this way for most of the other intermediate steps. For example, the electronic data files provided to us by the city do not distinguish those who received invitations for the interview from those who passed the interview. This information may exist in paper records of the interviewer rating forms, but we did not obtain access to those for this study. Similarly, those who complete the background investigation form are automatically rated in the Initial Panel Review, so there is no selection decision or applicant attrition between those two steps. Likewise, those who pass the Initial Panel Review automatically receive a background investigation, which is in turn automatically sent for Final Panel Review, so there is no selection decision or applicant attrition in those steps either.

Table 4.3
Number and Percentage Taking Versus Passing the Written Test, 2013 Applicant Cohort

	Total Invited to Take Written Test	Total Taking Written Test	Total Passing Test	Proportion Taking (Taking / Invited)	Proportion Passing (Passing / Taking)	Proportion Passing (Passing / Invited)
Race/ ethnicity						
White	5,509	4,008	3,274	73%	82%	59%
Hispanic	4,160	3,257	1,912	78%	59%	46%
Black	1,960	1,181	389	60%	33%	20%
Asian	869	671	524	77%	78%	60%
Native American	129	94	75	73%	80%	58%
Not Listed	609	406	330	67%	81%	54%
Gender						
Male	12,391	9,043	6,133	73%	68%	49%
Female	669	459	267	69%	58%	40%
Not Listed	176	115	104	65%	90%	59%
Total	13,236	9,617	6,504	73%	68%	49%

SOURCE: Los Angeles Personnel Department.

Table 4.4
Ethnic and Gender Differences in Rates of Passing the CPAT at the Orange County Testing Center, January 1, 2013–April 21, 2013

	Impact Ratio
Hispanic v. white	0.98
Black v. white	0.96
Asian v. white	0.98
Female v. male	0.63*

SOURCE: California Fire Fighter Joint Apprentice Committee.

* Indicates that the proportion passing is statistically different from the comparison group at $p < 0.05$.

tools as well, if the order of the test were changed. Because the composition of the group of applicants at the later stages is substantively different from that in the earlier stages, we cannot say whether the later stages would have shown disparate impact had the applicant pool not be restricted in that way.

Furthermore, in some race groups and in the female group, sample sizes were quite small in later stages (e.g., there were only 19 black applicants remaining at Stages 6 and 7 and 19 female applicants remaining at Stage 5, and the numbers were even smaller after that). This means that for those groups estimates of selection ratios in those later stages should be expected to be quite volatile. Were the exact same selection practices to be repeated on a completely new set of applicants, disparate impact ratios for those groups would likely be drastically different from those observed here in the later stages in the selection process. It is for exactly that reason that we also asterisk the selection ratios in Tables 4.2 and 4.3 that were statistically different from the comparison group (white or male applicants).

Statistical significance is important to consider here, but it too should be interpreted with caution. Statistical differences are harder to detect when sample sizes are small. Even large differences may not be statistically significant for very small groups. As sample size increases, the amount of difference that can be detected between two groups gets smaller. Hence, even very small and meaningless differences can be statistically significant when sample sizes are large.

For these reasons, we advise considering both the 80% rule and the statistical significance test when viewing the information reported here. A difference that is statistically significant but that does not violate the 80% rule (or come close to violating it) may not have practical significance in this case. Similarly, a test that violates the 80% rule but that does not show statistically significant differences also may not have practical significance, as estimates based on small sample sizes (such as those in the later stages for the black and female applicant groups) are simply too volatile to be soundly interpreted.

CHAPTER FIVE

Recommendations

As mentioned in Chapter One, the recommendations we make here draw heavily on our knowledge and experience in personnel selection and workplace diversity. They are informed not only by the professional guidelines for personnel selection practices described in the *Principles* (2003) and the *Standards* (2014) but also by the vast literature of applied and scientific research on the validity of tests in employment contexts, successful approaches to increasing diversity, recruiting best-practices, and firefighter selection practices.

Although we rely on that research literature and the professional practice guidelines, we tailor our recommendations specifically to the city's existing selection process and needs. To understand that process, we closely reviewed the process that the city had in place at the outset of this study (we reviewed the existing selection materials, we reviewed documentation supporting the validity of the materials, and we supplemented that information by interviewing city personnel to further clarify the processes). We also tailored the recommendations to address specific selection issues, needs, and goals expressed by the city and key stakeholders. Lastly we analyzed data on disparate impact and conducted interviews with firefighters to confirm the completeness of the existing job analysis information.

We present our recommendations based on the information we gathered from the review, informed by our knowledge of the literature and professional practice guidelines, and drawing on the information and analyses described in Chapters Three and Four and Appendixes A and B. Where relevant, we cite other literature or previous research that provides additional evidence for the recommendation.

First, we outline general approaches that will ensure that recommended improvements to the firefighter selection process meet each of the four objectives we defined in Chapter One. Next, we discuss several overarching recommendations related to recruiting, validating selection criteria, managing the size of the applicant pool, setting up a robust appeals process, and establishing minimums. We also discuss aligning content with existing job analyses and improving electronic documentation and use of online technology. Finally, we offer a number of specific suggestions for revising the firefighter selection process, organized by where candidates fit in the department's current ten-step process.

Overview of Recommendations as They Relate to the Objectives

As we stated previously, our effort to improve the firefighter selection process was guided by four objectives. In this section, we provide a brief overview of the recommendations as they relate to those objectives.

Objective 1: Identify Applicants Most Likely to Be Successful Firefighters

How can the city meet this objective? The city needs to directly link the firefighter selection criteria in each stage of the hiring process with the KSAOs that firefighters need to perform their tasks or with success in training and on the job. This process, called *validation*, is a well-established requirement for supporting legal defensibility of a selection practice (e.g., see the Equal Employment Opportunity Commission's *Uniform Guidelines*, 1978) and considered a best-practice in personnel selection (see the *Standards* and the *Principles*).[1] Validation is the process of establishing evidence that (1) the content in a selection test maps

---

[1] American Educational Research Association et al., 2014; and Society for Industrial and Organizational Psychology, Inc., 2003.

onto important aspects of the job (showing *content-related evidence of validity*), (2) the test measures what it is purported to measure (showing *construct-related evidence of validity*), and (3) the test predicts or is correlated with important job-related outcomes (showing *criterion-related evidence of validity*).[2] *Validity* of a selection practice is established by amassing multiple sources of these types of validity evidence. Validation is discussed further in Appendix A.

The Personnel Department has made several efforts to follow best practices. For example, in 2010 it sponsored a job analysis for the LAFD that systematically examined the tasks or activities that LAFD firefighters do as part of their job, including the knowledge, skills, and abilities they need to succeed. Conducting a job analysis, which is a well-established method for defining important and frequent tasks in a particular job, is the first step in validating a selection system. It serves as the foundation for all three types of validity evidence, in that it helps define precisely the tasks needed to perform the job (and the related KSAOs needed to perform those tasks successfully). Those tasks are ultimately what needs to be accurately predicted by the selection system. The analysis identified 18 overarching job duties (each with separate subtasks), ranging from ladder operations and sizing up a fire scene to emergency response and community relations. It also identified eight different overarching competencies (each with separate sub-competencies) that to varying degrees are required to perform each job duty. These competencies ranged from general cognitive abilities and thinking and reasoning skills, to written and oral communication, interpersonal skills, and physical abilities.

As a part of our research effort, RAND conducted interviews and focus groups to confirm and update the content of the 2010 job analysis. In general, we found that the bulk of the findings from the 2010 job analysis are still applicable; however, we also identified a few additional tasks not previously represented. Appendix B provides an overview of our findings in this area. Ultimately, the job analysis findings should

---

[2] Note that we define these here as three distinct types of validity evidence to simplify the concepts for our readers. For a more in-depth discussion of validity, see the *Standards* and the *Principles*.

be used as the basis for defining the different elements of the selection system to ensure that the most important KSAOs needed to succeed as a firefighter are assessed.

Although the Personnel Department's job analysis is a necessary and valuable first step in the process of collecting information to support validation efforts, more evidence is needed to fully confirm and document the connections between the selection criteria (and any relevant minimum standards) and the information from the job analysis. This is discussed in several places below.

Objective 2: Ensure Equal Opportunity[3] Throughout the Hiring Process

How can the city meet this objective? Among other things, it should follow best practices for ensuring fair treatment of applicants during the selection process. This includes establishing a systematic process in which all applicants are treated essentially the same. This can be accomplished by

- creating strict and concrete guidelines for interviewing, scoring, and investigating applicants
- providing training on and evaluating all administrators in their application of those guidelines
- providing all applicants with easy access to study and practice materials
- providing public access to as many details on the process as possible so applicants can prepare for it on their own
- ensuring that the process does not place unrealistic or disproportionately unfair time, scheduling, and cost burdens on applicants.

Later in this chapter, we discuss specific elements that could be changed in the current selection process to provide additional support for fairness at various stages in the process.

---

[3] We use the term *equal opportunity* here to make reference to the need to adhere to equal employment opportunity guidelines for selection practices and fair treatment in the hiring process.

Objective 3: Increase the Demographic Diversity of New Firefighter Hires

How can the city meet this objective? If the firefighter selection process is valid (that is, it addresses the first objective of deciding who will and will not be a good firefighter) and it affords applicants an equal opportunity of being hired (that is, it addresses the second objective of giving all individuals fair and equal treatment during the employment process), then the best way to accomplish this objective is with better recruiting. This will require the city to target firefighter outreach and recruiting efforts specifically toward minorities and women who are most likely to successfully complete the selection process. This is discussed in greater detail below.

Objective 4: Minimize Costs for the City of Los Angeles and Its Applicants

How can the city meet this objective? The cost of the firefighter hiring process is directly linked to both the number of applicants the Personnel Department needs to process and the efficiency of the process itself. Therefore, the city can minimize costs by identifying viable applicants early in the process and reducing duplicative steps in the selection process. In our review of the 2013 firefighter selection process, we identified significant overlap in Steps 3 through 9. Consolidating some of these steps could improve the efficiency of the selection process. Additionally, we recommend automating as many of the background screening elements as possible[4] and moving those automated screening steps further up in the process. This is explained further below.

---

[4]   See our recommendation to establish minimums on the background qualifications, discussed later in this chapter.

Overarching Recommendations Targeting the Four Objectives

Start a New Citywide[5] Outreach and Recruiting Campaign for the LAFD

Improving the diversity of the LAFD will require a long-term and carefully targeted outreach and recruiting campaign. The goal should be to maximize the number of highly qualified and highly competitive racial minority and female participants in the firefighter selection process. Given that recent negative media coverage of the firefighter hiring process may have exacerbated perceptions that the city is not committed to improving diversity, starting a new recruiting and outreach effort targeted at identifying highly qualified racial minority and female candidates would be a good first step to improving some of those negative public perceptions. The recommendations offered here are consistent with research findings on factors that should be addressed to make outreach and recruiting efforts successful.

Engage in Targeted Recruiting

As noted earlier, the initial applicant pool does show good racial and ethnic diversity; however, only a small proportion of those applicants had the necessary skills, abilities, and other characteristics to be highly competitive for the very small number of training openings. When the odds of selection are so low (regardless of minority membership) and when minority applicants are heavily recruited and still rejected at high rates, perceptions of unfairness may arise even when unfairness in the selection process does not exist. Research has shown that recruiting efforts that specifically target high-performing minority individuals are one of the best ways to help improve minority representation in the group selected (e.g., see Newman and Lyon, 2009). Moreover, considering the volume of applicants the Personnel Department already struggles to handle, recruiting more applicants without regard to their competitiveness can add to the Personnel Department's burden without much gain in diversity of the final selectees. For these reasons,

---

[5]   It could be useful to expand recruiting efforts to Los Angeles County and beyond, although that would likely entail expenditure of even more resources.

engaging in targeted recruiting is generally considered a good approach for organizations that want to boost minority representation among those who are ultimately selected.

Targeted recruiting efforts should actively seek out specific individuals who would add to the LAFD's demographic diversity and who are likely to be competitive recruits (e.g., are extremely physically fit, have exceptional records as model citizens, participate in community volunteer efforts, and have excelled academically). Examples of such targeted recruiting could include female athletes or minority valedictorians at local high schools; veterans; other fire departments; colleges; and high schools with Reserve Officer Training Corps (ROTC) or first-responder programs. The LAFD and Personnel Department will need to devise creative methods for identifying and reaching these groups and continuously explore the success of those methods through trial and error.[6]

The LAFD and the Personnel Department might also consider providing financial assistance or free training to selected applicants to help them meet certain minimum requirements that they could not otherwise meet without such assistance. For example, the expenses associated with meeting the requirements for CPAT and EMT certification may be prohibitive for low-socioeconomic-status populations. To address this, the city could consider, for example, offering subsidies for EMT tuition or the CPAT training courses described in Chapter Three, especially for those people who are highly competitive[7] on all of the other key selection factors.[8]

---

[6] Because many approaches should be explored and the success of those efforts can best be explored through trial and error, identifying and recommending specific groups to target and methods for recruiting them was not feasible within the 90-day time constraint for this study.

[7] Some sort of screening process for handing out these subsidies would be needed.

[8] Note that to offer this for all or even a large subset of the applicants would be cost prohibitive, so the city would need to implement a highly competitive selection process where people are carefully screened on the other selection process elements, prior to offering assistance.

Consider Using Fire Stations as Outreach Centers

The city might find value in asking members of fire stations to help conduct outreach within their local communities. If the city chooses to use fire stations in this way, the Personnel Department should consider providing in-depth training to some members of fire stations and certifying them as official recruiters. Those certified personnel could then serve as recruiting liaisons equipped to do more than simply direct interested people to the city's website or pass out fliers. This training could include providing clear guidelines on how firefighters should describe the minimum qualifications and what advice the firefighters could give to help people meet those qualifications or to make themselves more competitive.[9] Additionally, the LAFD firefighter recruiting unit could consider providing a minimum amount of recruiter training to all LAFD members by using webinars to disseminate educational materials describing firefighter recruiting policies and practices. This approach could reach many firefighters in a short period of time.

Expand the Capabilities of the Firefighter Recruiting Website

Although we did not do an in-depth examination of how the firefighter website could be improved, a quick scan of the information on that site suggests that more could be done in that area. Expanding the firefighter recruiting website (http://www.joinlafd.org/) would enable the LAFD to

- monitor trends in individuals who are interested in applying for firefighter positions
- post clear selection criteria, including minimum personal background characteristics, that can disqualify applicants or be used to deselect them[10]
- accept applications online and automate the initial screening process.

---

[9] Because of media concerns over nepotism in past hiring cycles, the city might be reticent to allow firefighters leeway in providing this advice. Clear guidelines for who could give such advice and how, would be needed.

[10] The city currently does not have such minimums in place. We have, however, recommended that the city establish some. This recommendation is discussed later in this chapter.

Currently, the Personnel Department collects the name, email, ethnicity, and sex of interested individuals (http://personline.lacity.org/notecard/). The firefighter recruiting website is also capable of collecting information for the purpose of tracking recruiting information.[11] Additional information about recruitment (such as where and how they learned about the firefighter hiring opportunities) could be useful for helping the city improve its outreach and recruiting efforts into diverse communities. If such recruiting information is not currently collected through the website, we suggest adding this capability. Although we recommend that the website ask for this information, applicants should be told that disclosing it is entirely voluntary, so they are not dissuaded from applying because of the request for such information.

More important, the firefighter recruiting website and the Personnel Department's website should post an expanded list of selection criteria. The websites should clearly describe what factors will exclude someone from qualifying and explain how each selection criterion is linked to KSAOs identified by the job analysis. As we have stated above, clear descriptions of selection criteria will effectively manage applicants' expectations, provide transparency in how the selection process operates, and promote public trust in the fairness[12] and effectiveness of the process (see Truxillo et al., 2009 and 2004, for more on the importance of this). Clear communication of what criteria or factors can disqualify applicants and lead to non-selection can also

---

[11] The city has some capability of tracking this additional information, however, we are not aware of what information is being tracked or whether that information is currently being used to improve the process.

[12] There are several ways in which tests can be perceived to be unfair, some of which may also lead to disparate impact. Lack of available resources for test preparation is one such example. If some applicants have resources available to study and practice for the test, and if such study and practice impact their performance on the test, then the availability of practice resources can make a difference for both perceptions of fairness and disparate impact. For example, if test prep resources are only available through for-profit test-prep firms (as is often the case), applicants without enough money may feel it is unfair to not have free access to such preparation. Additionally, lack of resources to pay for test prep typically affects racial groups differentially because of differences in socioeconomic status.

save the city's resources and applicants' expenses.[13] This could lead to fewer applicants disqualified by their personal history later in the background investigation process. In addition, the website should continue providing examples of written test questions for applicants to practice.

The Personnel Department website or the firefighter recruiting website, or both, should be able to accept applications online and process initial screening of applicants. The initial screening should go beyond the current minimum requirements and use an expanded list of selection criteria. It should provide disqualification notifications for applicants whose personal backgrounds prevent them from meeting the minimum selection criteria.[14] This capability will allow the Personnel Department to digitally track applicants' information and automate initial assessment of their personal background. (See below for more on the discussion of setting standards on background criteria and automating the initial stages of the selection process.)

Lastly, social media outlets could be explored further as sources of outreach and recruiting with special attention paid to sites that could lead to increases in highly qualified women and racial minorities. Success of the use of social media outlets for reaching these groups should be explored through trial and error.

---

[13] Providing accurate information summarizing the qualifications of people selected for training and those who graduate, and explaining how these qualifications relate to firefighter job performance could help provide applicants the chance to better understand why they might not make it past specific steps in the process. However, care should be taken to ensure that the information provided on the website is accurate and discusses valid firefighter job requirements and does not inadvertently disclose confidential information about people selected. Care should also be taken to ensure that that information does not have a detrimental chilling effect on applicants, where some highly qualified applicants decide not to apply. Applicant reactions to this type of information therefore should be evaluated first, before such changes are implemented.

[14] As all disqualifications must be appealable, this would require that an appeals process be available. Cost-effective means for handling those appeals would need to be devised.

Validate Selection Criteria by Establishing Relationships to KSAOs Required to Be an Effective Firefighter

We found that many elements of the current firefighter hiring process are consistent with best practices of personnel selection.[15] However, additional validation efforts are needed to provide evidence supporting the link between selection criteria and required KSAOs.[16] Depending on the types of criteria, the validation methods can vary. Additionally, multiple sources of evidence are needed to support the selection tools.

Validation Is Recommended Regardless of Disparate Impact

Efforts to validate selection practices are vital when disparate impact is observed. Although a selection practice may show disparate impact, that finding alone does not necessarily mean that its continued use is unlawful. In fact, practices that show disparate impact are not considered unlawful if they are job-related or tied to a business necessity and no other reasonable alternatives with less disparate impact are available.

A selection practice is considered discriminatory, however, if it shows disparate impact and the employer cannot provide sound evidence that it is job-related (see Appendix A for more on the importance of ensuring legal defensibility). This is one reason we recommend that systematic evidence be collected showing the link between the Personnel Department's selection criteria and important KSAOs on the firefighter job. Such evidence can justify the continued use of a selection practice known to show disparate impact.

Moreover, some practices can show disparate impact and still be an important predictor of success in the workplace. In such cases, an employer may ultimately decide to continue using the practices. In public safety jobs or in jobs where the public pays for costly training— both relevant to firefighter jobs—ensuring good prediction of performance on the job or in training may be very important. Similarly, practices that do not show disparate impact should still be validated,

---

[15] For example, rater training and highly structured scoring rubrics are recommended best practices (see the *Principles* and *Standards*).

[16] For example, it is generally considered best practice for interviews to be highly structured. Additionally, it is important for the content of interview questions to be based on information from a job analysis. Both appear to be the case in this instance.

as establishing job-relatedness is considered best practice in personnel selection regardless of disparate impact. Especially in public safety
jobs, it is vital to rely on selection criteria that have been shown to effectively distinguish candidates who are most likely to maintain public
safety from those who are not.

According to the extant research literature, many of the procedures showing disparate impact in Table 4.2 involve tools that are
generally supported as valid for predicting performance of firefighters
(such as the use of a structured interview and an aptitude test).[17] This
suggests that these tools may be valid in this instance and therefore
worth retaining in spite of their showing disparate impact. Additionally, because some of the selection tools applied by the city (e.g., the
interview) also involve highly structured and systematic processes, concerns about the possibility of some threats to validity (such as widely
varying interview questions or the use of untrained raters) are less-
ened. Nevertheless, there is still a need to validate the specific tools in
use by the Personnel Department to determine whether the tools show
adequate reliability and accuracy. This type of validation documentation for the Personnel Department's selection procedures is therefore
included in our recommendations.

In summary, efforts to validate selection practices are vital and
reflect a best practice regardless of whether they show disparate impact.
(For more on this, see the *Standards*.)

Explore Options for Reducing the Applicant Pool to a Manageable Size

In 2013, the number of firefighter applicants to the city dwarfed the
number of available positions. When the number of applicants becomes
excessive, the Personnel Department cannot allow everyone to move
through the selection process. Instead, the department uses a multiple-
hurdle system in which only those who pass a given hurdle are allowed
to continue on to the next step in the screening process. In 2013, this
approach resulted in disparate impact for key demographic groups.[18]

---

[17]   See Schmidt and Hunter, 1998.

[18]   See Chapter Four.

Therefore, the department should reevaluate the processes it uses to winnow down the number of applicants to a manageable size. In doing so, the city should pay particular attention to disparate impact (i.e., whether these processes affect the diversity of the applicant pool) and the validity of the tool and the minimums used in that winnowing.

In the 2013 hiring cycle, the Personnel Department used both the written test and CPAT submissions to help reduce the applicant pool to a manageable level. In the past, the department has established a minimum cut point on the written test, above which all applicants are eligible to continue on. However, far more people pass that minimum than the Personnel Department can process. In 2013, for example, more than 6,500 applicants passed the written test administered by the Personnel Department. To manage the vast number of applicants in 2013, the department opted for a "first come, first served" approach, in which only those applicants who submitted their CPAT certification in the first 60 seconds after the start of the filing period were allowed to continue. Although the approach of processing applications in the order in which they were received was announced in the job bulletin, it was still widely criticized as being unfair to applicants, and as shown in Chapter Four, it resulted in disparate impact for key demographic groups.

Although developing new minimums and outsourcing the written test are among our additional suggested changes (these are discussed in more detail in the appendixes), we suspect that the new minimums would still not reduce the applicant pool to a size that the Personnel Department could process for interviews. As a result, the Personnel Department will likely face a similar situation in the next hiring phase. We therefore discuss two approaches to reducing the number of applicants to a manageable level that do not suffer from the same problems as the "first come, first served" approach. Before we discuss those options, however, we offer a quick overview of the key challenges that the Personnel Department faces in making decisions about how best to narrow the applicant pool.

Aptitude Testing in Personnel Selection and Disparate Impact

There is a well-established finding that aptitude tests predict performance in a wide variety of workplace contexts. Aptitude tests consistently show good validity in predicting both job performance and training performance in a variety of workplace contexts (e.g., see Schmidt and Hunter, 1998), including in firefighter contexts (Barrett et al., 1999). In general, aptitude test relationships tend to hold across the range of aptitude test scores. As aptitude increases, so does performance in training and on the job (Schmidt and Hunter, 1998; Gottfredson, 2000). Aptitude tests are also easy to administer and score, which makes them relatively cost-effective and efficient. As a result, aptitude testing is a commonly used element in many large-scale selection efforts, including in firefighting contexts (see Appendix C for discussion of aptitude tests used by other fire departments).

However, employers and researchers for decades have repeatedly observed that aptitude tests have disparate impact on minority groups (e.g., see Ployhart and Holtz, 2008; Roth et al., 2001). Disparate impact is most commonly observed for Hispanic and black applicants, and in some cases for women. As a result, the use of aptitude tests can often lead to a less diverse group of selectees.

A number of researchers have documented the merits of various options for reducing disparate impact when using an aptitude test (e.g., see De Soete, Lievens, and Druart, 2013; Ployhart and Holtz, 2008). One of those options includes using multiple types of measures in a selection system in a compensatory system (rather than multiple hurdles). For example, in many organizational settings, employers seek to combine aptitude test scores with other selection criteria (such as interview ratings or non-cognitive tests) to arrive at a total score. The total score is then used for selection in a top-down fashion. This approach can help reduce disparate impact overall, but the gains are not typically enough to eliminate disparate impact, and in many cases the improvements in disparate impact are negligible. This is true in part because research typically does not support weighting personality as heavily as aptitude in the total score. Research has shown that certain personality traits can add modest amounts of incremental prediction over aptitude test scores, but they typically cannot be substituted for aptitude (e.g., see Schmidt and Hunter, 1998).[19] As a result, even when aptitude tests are combined with personality measures, selection decisions typically still show disparate impact (Ryan, Ployhart, and Friedel, 1998).

Because no clear solution to eliminating disparate impact on aptitude tests exists, we present two options for the city to consider for narrowing down the initial number of candidates, and both have distinct advantages and disadvantages.[20] The first option is to use top-down selection via aptitude testing, which does not solve the disparate impact issue. The second is to use random selection to preserve diversity representation through to the next phase in the selection process. The approaches are not mutually exclusive, and an effective selection process may involve a combination of both approaches.

Method 1: Top-Down Selection on the Written Test

If an organization places highest priority on maximizing performance outcomes without regard to impacts on diversity, it can justify a top-down selection process on an aptitude test, if higher scores on the test have been shown to relate to higher performance in job-related situations (such as success in job-related training). In other words, the Personnel Department could—if it had such evidence in support of the written test—select people in order of their scores to reduce the applicant pool to a manageable level. This is known as top-down selection.

If top-down selection is used, we recommend that the Personnel Department consider adding a non-cognitive personality measure to

---

[19] Two examples of potentially relevant personality traits are conscientiousness and extraversion. Conscientiousness has been shown to predict performance in a wide variety of jobs, and extraversion and other traits have been shown to predict performance in leadership positions (see, for example, Barrick and Mount, 1991; Judge et al., 2002). Personality-based integrity testing is also widely used in employment contexts and has been shown to predict a variety of counterproductive workplace behaviors (Ones, Viswesvaran, Schmidt, 1993).

[20] Legal issues should be factored into the decision of which method is most appropriate (see Appendix A for more discussion on this). Those legal issues are constantly evolving. Recent court cases involving aptitude tests that show disparate impact have added new complexities. Moreover, it is not clear how random selection practices would be received by the courts. We therefore recommend that the city's legal counsel advise them on which, if any, of these options is advisable in the current legal environment. See Appendix A for more discussion on this.

the written test and use a combined score for top-down selection.[21] A personality measure can help provide a more well-rounded assessment of the applicants. However, the inclusion of the personality measure would need to be supported with validity evidence.

In any case, as noted elsewhere in this report, any selection practice that has disparate impact must be shown to be valid for predicting important workplace outcomes. We expect that top-down selection for a written test similar to the one used in 2013 would show disparate impact,[22] so this option should be used only with tests that have been validated, with particular attention paid to documenting that higher scores are associated with better performance.

Method 2: Random Sampling[23]

To reduce disparate impact in the early stages of the selection process, the city might consider using random sampling rather than aptitude testing to reduce the initially very large applicant pool to a manageable level.[24] This approach would help preserve the diversity of the initial applicant pool, and it could be used in conjunction with a careful, rigorous, and valid applicant screening process to ensure that only highly qualified candidates receive offers.[25] The thoroughness of that subse-

---

[21] Personality traits such as conscientiousness or extraversion might be relevant in firefighter contexts, but validation evidence would be needed to support that hypothesis.

[22] Aptitude tests have been repeatedly shown to have disparate impact in many other employment settings (see, for example, Roth et al., 2001). Given that the written test showed disparate impact in 2013, we would expect similar findings on future tests like it.

[23] The use of a random sampling is something that the city asked RAND to examine. Our purpose in this section is not to recommend the use of random sampling, but rather to describe its advantages and disadvantages and to highlight issues for the city to consider if it does choose to use this approach.

[24] Sackett et al. (2001) notes that random selection is one extreme alternative to using an aptitude test if the goal is to reduce disparate impact in the selection process.

[25] We note that a random selection process used for narrowing the applicant pool would likely be viewed as a point where selection decisions are made. If an organization wanted all selection decisions to be valid (that is, they wanted the selection decisions to predict important workplace outcomes), then a random selection process would not be advisable. Thus this approach to winnowing the selection pool runs counter to advice suggesting that all selection decisions should be supported with validation evidence.

quent screening process would be especially important as public safety is a primary desired outcome of firefighter hiring.

However, while random sampling is one option for narrowing the applicant pool, we are aware of only one organization currently using such a system. To explore this, we contacted 20 large fire departments around the country; eight responded. Of those eight, three reported having tried random sampling[26] at some point in the past: the New York Fire Department in the 1980s and 1990s; the Oakland Fire Department in the 2000s; and the Chicago Fire Department as recently as their last hiring cycle, in 2006. Both New York and Oakland reported that the practice was discontinued, in part because the practice was generally disliked by applicants. Only Chicago reported a willingness to continue to use it (the city plans to use it again in its hiring cycle in the fall of 2014). Because applicant reactions to the process (for at least two of the departments trying it) were not positive, we strongly suggest that if the city attempts this method, the Personnel Department include a plan for making sure that applicants feel as fairly treated as possible in the process.[27] A broader census of departments to explore this process or its application in greater depth was not possible given the three-month time frame of this project.

The following are two random sampling procedures the Personnel Department could use to reduce the applicant pool. Each has advantages and disadvantages.[28]

---

[26] We did not inquire as to whether this included *stratified* random sampling or merely *simple* random sampling.

[27] It is worth noting that these anecdotes were from decades ago when the political and legal terrain was materially distinct. It is possible that in today's legal climate, applicant reactions could be different.

[28] Legal issues should be factored into the decision of which method is most appropriate. Those legal issues are constantly evolving. Recent court cases involving aptitude tests that show disparate impact have new complexities. Moreover, it is not clear how random selection practices would be received by the courts. We therefore recommend that the city's legal counsel advise them on which, if any, of these options is advisable in the current legal environment. See Appendix A for more discussion on this.

- **Option 1: Draw a simple random sample.** A simple random sample is essentially a "lottery" system in which every qualified applicant has the same odds of being selected. Selectees continue on in the process; those not selected do not continue. It is important to note that the demographic representativeness of a simple random sample will always vary from draw to draw due to chance alone (see Appendix D). Thus, the city could end up with a pool of random sample selectees that can be either more or less demographically diverse than the pool of people from which they were drawn.
- **Option 2: Draw a stratified random sample.** This procedure uses demographic characteristics to stratify the sample to increase the chances that it will have the same level of demographic diversity as the initial, larger pool. This "modified lottery system" gives every applicant the same odds of continuing on in the selection process as they had in the random process described above, but it utilizes demographic information from the applicants (see Appendix E for more on the mathematics of the process).[29]

Because the goal of random sampling is to narrow the applicant pool to a reasonable level, if random sampling is used, the random sample should be drawn early on in the selection process. However, we recommend doing as much prescreening as is practical in advance of a random selection process to help narrow the pool using merit- and qualification-based criteria. For example, in our step-by-step suggestions in the next section, we recommend automating some of the background checks and moving them to the first step in selection, before the written test. Elimination of greater numbers of applicants on the basis of this prescreening information could reduce some of the need for a random sampling method in the first place, and it could help improve the overall quality and competitiveness of the candidates ultimately chosen in the random sample.

---

[29] Note that use of a stratified sampling approach may lead some applicants to believe that they can game the system by falsely reporting they are a member of a particular racial group.

Take Care in Determining the Size of the Pool That Continues

Because the overall selection process relies on a multiple-hurdle system, the Personnel Department should keep in mind that for screening tools to be of use, they need to be able to continue to narrow the applicant pool. But for that to occur, there needs to be a sufficient number of applicants at later hurdle points to select from. This is especially important to consider when using a random or stratified random sample for selection, but it is also relevant when employing top-down selection on an aptitude test. If too few applicants are available to choose from after the earlier hurdles, the overall quality of the selectees could suffer in the end. The early sampling process could let through too many people who do not have the right qualities or skills to meet the interview and background standards criteria, and it may fail to let through enough candidates who would be considered high-quality and competitive in those later stages.

With too few applicants available later in the selection process, standards and expectations may have to be lowered in the later stages to result in enough selectees at the end of the selection process. To prevent that from occurring, we suggest that the Personnel Department seek to maximize the size of the applicant pool deemed "manageable." We also recommend that, regardless of the method used to reduce the pool to a manageable size, checks be in place to make sure that the resulting pool of individuals stays highly competitive through the later hurdles. If quality dips below a threshold, checks need to be in place to catch it.[30] In those cases, larger numbers of personnel would need to be allowed to move forward in the process to bring the quality of selectees back up to expectations.

---

[30] One way to check scoring would be to compare average scores from interviews and panel reviews across administrations. If scoring for those is highly structured and standardized with clear criteria for how to assign scores, dips in scores should be observed with declines in quality. If instead, scoring is highly subjective, dips in scores might not be observed. A way to check this would be to have raters rate a hypothetical applicant whose answers are written on paper. Using the same hypothetical paper, people across administrations could determine if scoring is consistent or instead inadvertently being adjusted based on the quality of the applicants.

Establish a Robust Appeals Process for Applicants Who Believe That They Have Been Wrongly Deselected

Having robust appeals procedures for applicants who believe they have been treated unfairly during the selection process or believe they were not selected because of some bias in the system will help build trust in the firefighter hiring process and minimize chances for costly litigations. This is particularly relevant in the context of those who were deselected in the process rather than disqualified (disqualified applicants are automatically entitled to appeal).

We also recommend taking steps not only to have an appeals process, but also to establish as much transparency and feedback as possible on the reasons for deselecting applicants. This is consistent with extensive literature on how perceived justice of organizational practices and procedures can be influenced by how much information and explanation individuals are given about those practices and procedures (e.g., see Colquitt et al., 2001). It is also consistent with recommendations stemming from research on applicant reactions to selection procedures (e.g., see Truxillo et al., 2004 and 2009; Smither et al., 1993).

There already is an appeals process in place for candidates who fail parts of the application process. The only part of the process not appealable is the panel review processes, where instead of a "fail" result or disqualification, candidates are non-selected or deselected because they are not the most competitive. We would recommend adding an appeals process for this non-selection process as well, particularly given the subjective nature of the panel reviews and the current lack of transparency for what constitutes an applicant's competitiveness. The city has noted, however, that resources would be a big concern if appeals for panel review were implemented.

We nevertheless recommend that the city set aside funding and resources for communicating the reasons for cutting applicants and for handling complaints. We recommend including opportunities for retesting and instituting procedures for when initial interviewer ratings show discrepancies, suggesting a concern in inter-rater reliability. In such cases, for example, the original interview could be reviewed and re-scored by new sets of interviewers (assuming they are taped or transcribed). If it appears that the questions themselves were not well-suited to the applicant's situation, the applicant could be re-interviewed. The firefighter recruiting website should post information about such opportunities for retesting or re-scoring. It should also post the criteria for appeals, including a description of what packages of information may be necessary to submit to initiate appeals. The results of the appeals process should provide clear guidelines that spell out how individual applicants can improve and how they can meet selection criteria. These recommendations are consistent with suggested best practices for selection processes used in high-stakes employment decisions (e.g., see the *Standards,* pp. 56–57).

Increase Electronic Documentation and Use of Online Technology During the Selection Process

Improvements in recordkeeping technology could offer several benefits. Electronic documentation would allow for quick submission and retrieval of information at various steps in the process. Electronic recordkeeping could serve to streamline the selection process by allowing easier access to information about applicants and eliminating the need for staff to process applicant information by hand.

Currently the entire background check is paper-based. The LAFD has only recently moved to emailing reference-check information to an applicant's listed references; however, the results of the reference checks are still relegated to a paper file. Instead, gains could be made by using an online process for the people listed as references, for example, to submit their reference-check information, and for background investigators to submit their results. This could potentially allow for the non-selection of personnel at an earlier point in the process (as soon as information is obtained that meets non-select criteria, a suggestion discussed further in Step 1 below). Information could also easily be shared and cross-referenced across personnel conducting background checks, interviewers, and personnel responding to appeals.

Moreover, electronic documentation allows for more flexibility in double scoring and in examining the reliability and validity of the process and disparate impact of certain elements in the background investigation. For example, all the scores—not just the final overall score—assigned by members of the panel review team and their scores for each dimension could be recorded electronically. Doing so would allow sub-score information to be validated against future performance, leading informed revisions to improve the panel review content.

Although moving to electronic recordkeeping would be initially costly, the long-term gains will likely outweigh the initial costs.

Align the Content in Each Selection Step with the Job Analysis and Deconflict It with Other Elements in the Process

Each selection method should be designed so as to not be inadvertently duplicative of other methods. Instead, any duplication that is occurring should be by design, to either check the information, increase the reliability of the information, or measure the information in a way that increases the comprehensiveness of the dimension being measured. For example, the interview should focus on factors that are difficult to otherwise measure or to judge in other ways, whereas the background checks could be designed to verify some of the information obtained through the interview or other sources. Interviews should be designed to supplement rather than overlap with the information obtained during the background investigation steps.

At present, it appears that there is significant overlap in several steps of the process. Interview specialists interview candidates about the information in their PIQ and PHF (Step 6) after different interviewers interview the candidate in Step 5. In Step 7, new raters evaluate the PIQ and PHF information collected by the interviewers in Step 6. In Step 8, a background investigator compiles information on the candidate. In Step 9, an entirely new set of raters rate the information collected by the background investigator.

Consolidating some of these steps could speed up the review process and reduce the reliance on firefighter and Personnel Department staff. If firefighters still desire involvement in the decision process, some could be trained in the rating processes and asked to double-code a random subset of the investigations to determine whether their ratings agree with the investigators'. If they provide similar ratings to the investigators, there is no need to have them participate for all candidates. If they do not provide similar ratings, then until they do, the rating process and/or the training should be revised using existing job analysis information.

Tie Minimums on All Selection Factors to Acceptable and Unacceptable Performance in Training or on the Job

For example, in the interviews, although a score of 70 is considered passing, candidates must score above 95 to move forward, unless there are too few high-scoring candidates. Similarly, on the final panel reviews, candidates move forward in the process based on their scores and the number of candidates needed. Although it is possible that candidates rated "Satisfactory" meet all of the qualifications necessary to be a successful and dependable firefighter, overall ratings of "Good" theoretically represent the minimum cutoff, and only candidates rated "Outstanding" by both raters were allowed to move forward in the last cycle. This top-down approach to selection can be justified if there is evidence suggesting that the applicants receiving the highest scores are in fact more likely to be successful firefighters.

Meaningful minimums for ratings should be set by tying scores to key job outcomes and job requirements. The minimums should be set such that candidates at that rating or above are indeed likely to perform well and meet other needs. If candidates are being held to a higher standard (such as by the use of top-down selection where only the highest scorers are offered employment), those higher standards should be checked for validity and disparate impact. We recommend that the city establish minimums that are tied to job requirements.

Step-by-Step Recommendations for Improving the Selection Process

Our review of the existing firefighter selection practices suggests that some of the criteria and methods used are well supported in the existing literature on best practices for personnel selection (including the use of an aptitude test, a structured interview, and background checks). However, reliance on research conducted in other contexts on selection tools that are not the same as the ones used by the Personnel Department is not sufficient to defend the use of these tools. Instead, the Personnel Department should collect additional information using its own selection test information and its own applicant, training, and incumbent populations to further support the continued use of these selection processes.[31]

In this section, we point to some areas in the selection process that require more documentation of validity evidence, and offer suggestions below to provide additional theoretical and empirical support for the reliability and validity of the selection practices. We also offer specific suggestions for improving the selection process by promoting transparency, managing applicants' expectations, and helping to identify viable and competitive applicants early on in the process so as to improve efficiency and save resources for the city as well as its applicants.

We have organized the suggestions in this section according to where they fit in the firefighters' 2013 ten-step selection process, although, as we explain, we suggest that some steps in the process could be combined. In addition, we have three suggestions that span multiple steps.

Our suggested alternative hiring process consists of seven steps, as shown in Table 5.1, which is displayed against the current process for reference. Below, we discuss recommended changes relating to each of the existing 2013 process steps.

Suggested Changes to Step 1: Preliminary Background Application and Step 2: Minimum Requirements
Encourage Applicants to Submit All of Their Application Materials Online

Moving further toward a completely digital application process will improve the efficiency of the hiring process. Currently, initial applications are processed exclusively electronically; however, in the 2013 process, other parts of the process were not. For example, CPAT scores were allowed to be submitted in paper form as well. Applicants should

---

[31] A study collecting criterion-related validity evidence that covered this was conducted in 1996. However, the test used in the 2013 administration did not contain the same test items as the one studied in 1996. The city has indicated that the study could be completed again.

Table 5.1
Suggested Alternative Firefighter Hiring Processes for the LAFD

2013 Process	Suggested Alternative
Step 1: Preliminary Background Application	Step 1: Expanded Online Application
Step 2: Minimum Requirements	Step 2: Physical Prescreener
Step 3: Written Test	Step 3: Written Test
Step 4: CPAT	Step 4: CPAT
Step 5: Oral Interview	Step 5: Interview and Background Investigation
Step 6: Background Investigation and Preliminary Investigative Questionnaire	Step 6: Medical and Psychological Examinations Final Review
Step 7: Initial Panel Review	Certification
Step 8: Field Investigation	
Step 9: Final Panel Review	
Step 10: Medical and Psychological Exams	
Certification	

be allowed to submit paper copies of that type of information, but they should be warned that the hard-copy submission will take longer to process. Applicants can already access and submit the application at locations throughout the city (such as public libraries) where members of the public can connect to the Internet. By further automating the online process, information could be presented that allows applicants to better judge how their own qualifications stack up against those with whom they will be competing.[32]

---

[32] Providing accurate information summarizing the qualifications of people selected for training, those who successfully graduate training, and explaining how these qualifications relate to firefighter job requirements could help give applicants the chance to better understand why they might not make it past specific steps in the process. However, care should be taken to ensure that the information provided on the website is accurate and discusses valid firefighter job requirements and does not inadvertently disclose confidential information about people selected. Additionally, care should be taken to ensure that that information does not have a detrimental chilling effect on applicants, where some highly qualified appli-

Expand the Amount of Information Collected and Use It to Further Screen People

The application should collect an expanded list of relevant information (currently collected as preliminary background application, PIQ, and personal background history) that will determine whether applicants meet the minimum selection criteria. Applicants would be required to answer all questions and certify that the information they enter into the application is true. After minimums have been established by the city (as none currently exist), we recommend using them to eliminate or non-select applicants from continuing on in the process.

Conduct Electronic Background Checks During This Step

The application should collect necessary waivers for the Personnel Department to conduct electronic screening of applicants' backgrounds, including credit history and driving checks. These checks are relatively inexpensive and should be made during this step. For example, credit reports cost approximately $7 per person, and Department of Motor Vehicle records are provided at no charge (although costs in DMV labor is unknown). Both could be ordered early in the selection process and used to prescreen personnel for later steps. Doing so would require automation of the process, however, as reviewing these documents manually is labor-intensive.

Inform Applicants Who Do Not Qualify

The online application system should be programmed to inform applicants who do not meet minimum selection criteria that they have been disqualified. By putting this step first, it will help ensure that applicants who would be disqualified later do not proceed further.[33]

---

cants decide not to apply. Applicant reactions to this type of information therefore should be evaluated, before such changes are implemented.

[33] Note that this is already in place for some minimum qualifications, but minimums are not in place for the background standards. If background standards were used to disqualify or non-select personnel, then it would require validation of the minimums.

Suggested Changes to Step 3: Written Test
Outsource the Written Test to a Private Vendor That Has Validation Evidence to Support the Test, or Validate the Test Developed In-House

In 2013, the Personnel Department used a test comprising items developed and selected in-house. That test, although appearing to be similar in content to that of validated tests in use elsewhere, has not itself been subject to rigorous validation efforts. We recommend that the Personnel Department either validate its test content and establish minimum scores using a standard setting methodology consistent with the best practices outlined in the *Standards* and *Principles*, or outsource the administration of the entry-level firefighter exam to a private vendor. Outsourcing to a private vendor has a number of advantages over in-house test development and administration. Private vendors commonly conduct content and predictive validation studies to determine the efficacy of their tests, which can aid in legal defensibility of the tool, especially if selection occurs in a top-down fashion. Additionally, private vendors that specialize in test making often use experienced professionals, such as industrial/organizational psychologists and subject-matter experts, to produce relevant test questions that can identify the best firefighters for the job. Depending on the chosen vendor, the city potentially can avoid substantial expenditures connected with developing and administering the test that it would incur otherwise. Depending on the chosen private vendor, applicants can use the test scores to qualify for other fire departments that use the same vendor. With some vendors, applicants may be charged a testing fee. Grants should be available for applicants who demonstrate a financial hardship (qualification could be automatic based on their answers in the earlier background information step).

Appendix C provides examples of private vendors specializing in firefighter selection. In choosing a vendor, the Personnel Department should consider the following elements:

- Test content: the extent to which the test measures content relevant to the knowledge, skills, and abilities needed to be a firefighter

- Test development: the information and methods used to develop the test content, particularly, the extent to which the test was based on information from a job analysis
- Validity and reliability: the extent to which there is research evidence for the validity and reliability of the tests (i.e., the relationship between the test and important job performance criteria)
- Test administration: options for who administers it and how it is administered
- Availability of different test versions: the number of different available versions of the test[34]
- Administration costs: cost to the Personnel Department and applicants for using and taking the test, respectively
- Availability of study materials: the extent to which the vendor provides study materials to help applicants prepare for the test
- Inclusion of non-cognitive-personality measures (when combined with aptitude tests, non-cognitive measures can form a more comprehensive picture of the applicant at a very early stage in the process and possibly lead to some improvement in retention of minority applicants).[35]

Regardless of whether the test is outsourced or validated in-house, the city still needs to establish minimum passing scores using a formal method (such as convening panels to set standards) supported by best practices in personnel research (as noted above), and to carefully document the results (see the *Standards* and *Principles* for more on this).[36]

---

[34] No specific number of versions is needed; however, the existence of multiple versions allows for retesting and ensures test security to prevent cheating from one administration to the next. The more versions available, the more secure the test content and the more chances for retesting.

[35] For more on combining cognitive and non-cognitive predictors, see Schmidt and Hunter, 1998.

[36] Note that their current method for setting the minimum standards is to adjust it to a level that does not lead to too much disparate impact. We recommend instead, tying the minimum to requirements in training and on the job.

Suggested Changes to Step 4: Candidate Physical Ability Test
Consider Prescreening Applicants for the CPAT Before Allowing
Them to Take the Written Test

The CPAT is costly for applicants (currently around $150), and administering and scoring the written test for applicants who are unlikely to pass the CPAT is wasteful for both the city and applicants. Administering a physical pre-screener might help address this issue by ensuring that only the individuals who are most likely to also pass the full CPAT move on to take the written test. Then, only applicants who pass the written test would move on to take the full CPAT.

The pretest could require applicants to complete Event 7 of CPAT, the rescue/dummy drag, which requires candidates wearing a 50-pound vest to drag a 165-pound dummy for 70 feet. The Personnel Department and the LAFD could offer the prescreener throughout Los Angeles. Charging a nominal fee for the pre-test (such as $15)[37] could help cover the staffing costs and prevent people from testing who are not serious about the job. Such test fees could be credited toward a discount price on their official CPAT, if they make it to that point in the selection process.

Although using a prescreener could be considered, we note that according to the information provided to us by the CPAT testing company 94 percent of those who take the CPAT pass it. As a result, this could be a wasted effort if it serves to eliminate only 6 percent of applicants.

Collect Data on Applicants' CPAT Results

The physical test (the CPAT) is already outsourced to the California Fire Fighter Joint Apprentice Committee. The benefits of outsourcing the test to this particular vendor is that the CPAT possesses such obvious content and face validity that it is unlikely to face a successful legal challenge. The downsides to outsourcing include the costs to participants and the inability to set a different minimum standard on performance, as the test is pass/fail only. We recommend, however, that the

---

[37] This is a nominal amount that most applicants could afford; however, to prevent disparate impact, waivers could be offered.

Personnel Department start requesting pass and fail information on all applicants and examine the disparate impact and predictive validity of the test. Data on testing times and other scores for each event during the test should be requested as well.

Reserve a Block of Testing Times and Provide Transportation to and from Testing Sites

Because CPAT testing takes time, and appointments may not be available to accommodate many test-takers, we recommend that the city negotiate that the CPAT testing facility set aside a block of testing times that spans several weeks to accommodate applicants at the relevant time in the selection process. That will ensure that all applicants have a chance to take the test within the required time period. The city also should ensure that a variety of testing times are made available within that testing window, that there is sufficient time to complete and submit the test scores, and that there are reasonable options for transportation to and from the testing sites (as testing sites are located far away).

Suggested Changes to Step 5: Oral Interview, Step 6: Background Investigation and Preliminary Investigative Questionnaire, and Step 8: Field Investigation

Combine These Three Steps

To streamline the process, we recommend that the oral interview and the background interview and field investigations be conducted at the same time, and that a team of two city representatives as evaluators be assigned to each candidate for this entire combined step. These two evaluators would conduct and score the interview and the background and field investigations.

Use Personnel Department Staff as Evaluators, with LAFD Officials Providing Expertise and Independent Assessments

To improve efficiency and consistency, we recommend that the evaluators be drawn from Personnel Department staff. The LAFD senior officials should, however, be involved in developing selection criteria and evaluating the reliability and accuracy of interviews and background investigations. For example, LAFD representatives should be asked to attend a small subset of interviews, review those applicants' background information, and provide independent ratings of the candidates. Those ratings should be compared to the ratings the Personnel Department's team of evaluators provided on the same candidates to gauge the reliability and accuracy of the procedure. Rater drift should also be examined periodically and recalibration training should be implemented as needed.

Further Standardize Interview Procedures

We also recommend that the Personnel Department develop methods to ensure that raters follow consistent procedures for interviews. As described in Chapter Three, interviews already follow a relatively set format, and the scoring system is highly standardized. Interviewers use a scorecard to rate candidates on each of the eight competencies and assign an overall score. The scorecard gives rating criteria in each of four ratings, with scores from 65 to 100: "unfavorable evidence" (65), "minimal favorable evidence" (70–79), "favorable evidence" (80–89), and "very favorable evidence" (90–100). Examples are provided to guide the interviewer's judgment. Very favorable evidence, for example, includes "Broad expectations/understanding of accomplishment in position" and "Experience beneficial to performance of duties/responsibilities." Although interviewers are given criteria, and the training provides a few example answers, rules specifying the exact behaviors that are unacceptable is not provided. Two raters may not interpret "Experience beneficial to performance of duties/responsibilities" the same; an example answer linked to the criterion might lead to more reliable scores. In addition, the weighting of scores is subjective. A rating of "unfavorable evidence" in any competence area leads to a failure overall, but absent this, the final rating of a candidate is an overall judgment rather than a weighted average or sum. Increasing the structure of both the interpretation of criteria and the weighting of scores could help improve reliability and accuracy of scoring.

As another example of how the interview process could be further standardized, the Personnel Department can implement a procedure that requires each interviewer to independently rate the applicant, and to save and record those scores. After individual scores are recorded, interviewers can compare their ratings and arrive at a consensus (as they do now). If unable to do so, a second panel of two city representatives can be convened to interview the applicant independently and serve as a tiebreaker.

Further Standardize the Background/Field Investigation Process

The background investigation process appears to be less standardized than the other processes, and much of the process is not codified in instruction manuals or training materials. The investigations are currently very thorough, but the process could be more structured, with greater consistency in the type and amount of information obtained on the applicants. For example, finding adverse events in someone's history prompts additional in-depth background checks. Instead, the same depth of a check could be applied to all candidates, with specific guidelines on when additional information should be pursued to clear the adverse events and when enough information on the candidate has been obtained. The intent of this change is twofold. First it would serve to limit the amount of time and resources that are spent on candidates with adverse events in their past. Second, it would help equalize the intrusiveness of the process and the amount and type of behavioral data obtained across candidates. Alternatively, if there is reason to not use the same depth and process for everyone, it should be clearly documented.

Document Background Investigation Training Procedures

Although background investigators and interview specialists receive in-depth training, the training materials are not codified in an official document. Such official documentation can help ensure efficiency, transparency, and consistency across personnel and administrations. Training for interviewers and panel reviewers is documented in official manuals, whereas training for the background investigators is not.

Institute Reliability Checks

Reliability checks should be added to the interview, background investigation, and PIQ processes. Those checks should be designed to regularly confirm that the training and structure are having the desired effect on the reliability and accuracy of the ratings. They should also be used to identify raters in need of remedial training and to identify changes needed in the training and structured processes to help ensure better reliability in the future.

Align Interview and Background/Field Investigation Standards with Job Analysis Information

As described in Chapter Three, the factors examined during these processes were developed by the Personnel Department in 2012. They are listed in Table 5.2.

The interview factors were developed to align with the areas defined in the most recent job analysis. These should be compared to those used in the background investigation, and links to the job analysis should be documented in the same way. Elements that cannot be directly tied to job requirements should be eliminated. For example, although the use of a military bonus of five points is imposed by the City Charter, it may introduce disparate impact for women. Many of the skills learned in the military may lead to better qualifications for firefighting, but we should expect those skills to also lead to higher scores in the interview, without need of a bonus. We recommend reconsidering the use of bonus because of its potential for disparate

Table 5.2
Factors Evaluated in the Background Investigations and Interviews

Background Standards	Interview Competencies
Interpersonal skills, sensitivity and respect for others	Job motivation
Decisionmaking and judgment	Initiative in learning
Maturity and discipline	Practical orientation
Honesty, integrity, and personal ethics	Adaptability
Setting and achieving goals	Service orientation
Record checks	Teamwork
	Respect for others
	Oral communication

NOTES: Although these background standards are specified in official documentation, their links to job requirements are not made explicit. We recommend taking steps to align the standards with the job analysis information by clearly specifying how each standard relates to activities required on the job. This alignment should be documented and used to guide the minimums set for behaviors that should lead to a non-select decision. If candidates are to be selected on the basis of these background standards, the relative importance of each standard should be determined by the job analysis. Scores for each standard should then be used to establish appropriate weighting for determining scores in each dimension.

impact. Note, however, that because this practice is mandated by the City Charter, a change to the City Charter would be required for it to be implemented.

Similarly, it is not initially obvious how some of the information asked in the PIQ and PHF (and other information collected during the background check) relates to job requirements. The links should be made explicit and documented. If they cannot be made, the items should be removed from the questionnaires and not be pursued in the background investigation process.

Conversely, elements that are not addressed anywhere in the selection process should be added into at least one of the selection process parts. For example, the ability to work and remain clear-headed under pressure has been described during our focus groups as one of the most important characteristics of a good firefighter. This is not currently measured in the selection process, but it could be explicitly addressed in the interview.

Suggested Changes to Step 7: Initial Panel Review and Step 9: Final Panel Review

As noted earlier in the chapter, there seems to be overlap in the content obtained in the interview, the background and field investigations, and the initial and final panel reviews. As such, we believe that a single panel review may be sufficient.

The panel rating process is also highly standardized in ways that are very similar to interviewer ratings. We therefore recommend making small improvements, such as adding structure to the assignment of overall scores and providing concrete examples of how to use each criterion in assigning ratings.

Suggested Changes to Step 10: Medical and Psychological Evaluations

More could be done to document links between the psychological and medical criteria and the job requirements outlined in the recent job analyses. More could also be done to examine reliability and consistency in the decisions made as a result of the medical and physical screening process. Additionally, there appears to be some confusion about the role of the background screening relative to the medical screening process. Some of the people we spoke with suggested that part of the field investigation and the background interviews (Steps 8 and 6 respectively) may be intended for use by the medical and psychological personnel; however, the medical personnel and the psychologists are not aware of which parts of the background check, if any, have that intent. This lack of clarity suggests that more could be done to specify a clear purpose for each element of the background investigation (Steps 6 and 8). If such elements are intended for use by medical personnel or psychologists, they should be clearly communicated and carefully designed and validated to meet their needs.

Key Considerations in Evaluating the Selection Process

Validity and Reliability

It is always in the best interest of an employer to ensure a reliable and valid selection process. This affords three benefits: (1) it assures the employer that those selected are more likely to perform well on the job than those not selected; (2) it allows for a legally defensible process; and (3) it is fair to applicants. Best practices in personnel selection require amassing evidence that each selection tool used provides reliable and valid measurements of job applicants.[1]

Reliable selection tools are those that are likely to produce the same scores about applicants regardless of where or when[2] the measurement took place, or who scored or who conducted the test. Valid selection tools are tools that distinguish the applicants that are more likely to be successful on the job (or achieve some other important job outcome) from the ones less likely to be successful. The more valid a tool, the fewer mistakes it makes when making that distinction. The more valid a tool, the better it is at identifying who would succeed on the job.

---

[1] Any point in a selection process where some people are allowed to continue and some are not is a point where a selection decision is made. Hence, we refer to any judgments, criteria, tests, or scores used to make those decisions as selection tools. The written test, the interviews, the panel reviews, etc., are all being used as selection tools in this context.

[2] Measurements should be stable across time, assuming someone's underlying capabilities have not changed. However, training, acquisition of new knowledge, or gains in experience could be expected to lead to changes in candidates' underlying capabilities across time.

There is no silver bullet that ensures reliability or validity. However, there are key features that can be put in place to help make both more likely.

Methods for increasing reliability include establishing highly structured processes for all steps and conducting reliability checks. To establish structure, training on how to conduct each part of the selection process should be provided and documented. Clear instructions, rules, and guidelines for how to provide any subjective ratings should be established. Anchoring ratings with behavioral examples and holding training sessions where raters practice applying the rating scale and receive corrective feedback on the accuracy of their ratings is also important. Additionally, checks on reliability help ensure the structure is serving its purpose. To check interviewer reliability, for example, interviewers can be asked to independently rate the same person without discussing their ratings. This can be done for several candidates and scores can be compared. To check whether performance by the same person varies drastically depending on the interview question, candidates can be asked multiple questions and their answers to each can be scored independently. Then their scores on each question can be compared.

Methods for increasing validity of a selection tool start with alignment of the selection process with a well-designed job analysis. KSAOs identified in the job analysis that cannot be easily trained and are either important or frequently needed in entry-level assignments on the job should be considered for inclusion in the personnel selection process. Once the key factors to be assessed are identified, tools supported in the existing research literature should be identified to address each factor. Tools with good existing support should be analyzed to examine ideally at least two forms of validation evidence: *predictive* (how well it predicts outcomes considered relevant to the job, such as training success, job performance, or injuries) and *content* (how well independent expert judges agree about the tool's content alignment with the factors identified in the job analysis). Examination of *predictive validation* evidence is ideally conducted as a pilot study where the tools are administered to applicants and those applicants are followed over time. In addition to examining both types of evidence, disparate impact, possible differential prediction, and the extent to which observed relationships are underestimates (because low performers have already been eliminated) are examples of key factors that should be examined before the tool is implemented and used for employment decisions.

Other Factors to Consider When Designing a Selection System

After ensuring the validity and reliability of the selection process, it is critical to consider other key factors when designing the process. For example, with the 2013 applicant cohort, about 13,000 people submitted applications for just 70 slots—which far exceeded the LAFD's firefighter hiring needs. The Personnel Department was therefore faced with the difficult job of winnowing down the applicant pool and identifying who would receive offers of employment. In deciding how to winnow down the pool, there are numerous factors that need to be weighed and considered, some involve constraints on how the city can process applications received. We discuss some of these key factors in more detail below.

The Value of Diversity
Organizations value increasing diversity for a variety of reasons, many related to social justice. Public safety personnel commonly serve as important role models for children and young adults in the community. Having more members of underrepresented groups visible to youth could help change stereotypes and encourage members of the underrepresented groups to follow the same career paths. There are also social benefits internal to the organization; that is, as numbers of underrepresented groups increase, the feeling of tokenism diminishes for members of those groups. The higher the number of highly competent personnel who are members of those groups, the more it contradicts negative stereotypes about the groups within the organization. In time, as the number of qualified personnel increases, the numbers who qualify for leadership positions will also increase. This will allow even

more members of the underrepresented groups to serve as role models, mentors, and leaders for personnel from all groups.

Social justice, however, is not the only reason for valuing diversity. In a public safety job, increasing diversity could have positive impacts on the organization's effectiveness. The public's views of the public safety personnel are shaped, in part, by their views on how well the personnel appear to represent the members and interests of the people within that community. When an organization appears less diverse than the community it serves (or the number of visible personnel appears to be disproportionately from one race or gender group), the public may develop a distrust of the organization and the personnel within it. If there is a perception that public safety personnel are incapable of relating to members of the community, it could lead to meaningful difficulties in serving that community.

Pressure from the community to increase the diversity of the LAFD offers evidence that some community members would support efforts to address social justice issues in the department. It is not clear, however, whether the current level of diversity of the LAFD has any impact on its ability to serve the community.

Costs to the City

All stages of the selection process are costly, including recruitment, test administration, interviews, background investigations, and medical and psychological examinations, particularly at the scale of 13,000 applicants. For example, maintaining an active recruitment campaign requires funding for events such as job fairs, recruitment materials, and time spent by firefighters and Personnel Department staff. In the past cycle, the Personnel Department had a budget of $105,000 for outreach and recruitment alone.

The costs associated with the written test are also substantial. In the last cycle, the cost to rent the Convention Center to accommodate the large number of test takers was roughly $20,000. The Personnel Department estimates that proctors cost about $6,000 on top of that. Test development, scoring, and recording of results are front-end and back-end expenses that also factor into implementing the written test, though exact costs for development and scoring have not been reported.

Interviews and background investigations, however, are the most expensive elements of the selection process because of the number of personnel hours required to complete them. In 2012–2013, almost 1,000 candidates were interviewed. The Personnel Department estimates the cost of interview specialists during the interview process at $6,000 and estimates the entire background investigation process, including clerical support and case managers, at upward of $270,000.

The city must also compensate city physicians and psychologists for medical and psychological examinations. The cost is currently mitigated because the number of candidates making it to these stages of the selection process is quite small. During the latest hiring cycle, the city Personnel Department estimates these examinations were a $10,000 expense.

LAFD staffing costs are not included in any of these estimates. Firefighters participate in the Initial Panel Review, the Final Panel Review, and oral interviews—these are additional responsibilities for firefighters who are often already working overtime. The Personnel Department, likewise, must dedicate its own staff outside normal hours for tasks like proctoring the written exam.

Finally, litigation associated with the city's hiring practices is a significant cost that must be considered. We discuss legal defensibility later in this appendix.

Costs Borne by the Applicant

All applicants are required to pay $150 for their CPAT testing. Candidates are also responsible for covering transportation costs for trips to the Personnel Department, the Convention Center, and to one of the CPAT testing facilities located outside the city. This does not include implicit costs associated with missing work, childcare, etc. Considering how to minimize the impact of these activities on the costs to the applicant are important goals for ensuring fairness to individuals in the process.

Additionally, some applicants pay to take courses (like the ~$10,000 paramedic course administered at the University of California, Los Angeles) or hire outside consultants (typically retired firefighters) for test preparation and interview advice. Steps should be taken to ensure that these types of activities do not unfairly advantage those who have the financial means to pay for them.[3] Examples of ways to help prevent this include offering access to free test preparation and interview advice similar to what is provided by paid consultants. Consideration could also be given to not requiring paramedic training or to not giving preference to those candidates who have such training.

Legal Defensibility

As we noted in the preface, it is not the intention of this report to offer legal advice or legal strategy. However, any recommendations for hiring practices should take into consideration some key issues associated with employment law. For that reason, some minimum discussion of those issues is necessary. This section introduces the concept of fair and lawful treatment of members of protected groups.

Under Title VII of the Civil Rights Act of 1964 (as amended by the Civil Rights Act of 1991), it is unlawful to engage in a hiring practice that intentionally discriminates (called disparate treatment) or inadvertently discriminates (called disparate impact) against members of a protected group (defined by race, color, sex, national origin, or religion),[4] unless the practice is job-related and consistent with business necessity. The determination of disparate treatment is based on the intentions and motives of the employer or individuals involved in the hiring process.

Disparate impact, in contrast, can occur irrespective of intent. It is instead determined on the basis of several types of statistical evidence, one of which is known as the 4/5ths rule (or the 80% rule).[5]

---

[3]   Examining the effects of those courses on applicant interview scores would be one way to determine if the courses offer an unfair advantage. If the courses falsely inflate scores such that people do better in the interview, but not better in training or on the job, then explore ways to make the selection process less susceptible to that type of coaching. If it increases both scores and later performance in training or on the job, then consider offering everyone similar course materials online for free.

[4]   Other characteristics (such as sexual orientation) are protected under local and state laws.

[5]   Although several federal agencies have adopted this rule, no federal court has adopted it as the definitive rule. Courts approach it on a case-by-case basis. Some courts have criticized it, and others have outright rejected it in favor of other rules.

Employment practices that violate the 4/5ths rule—that is, that result in a selection ratio for a protected group that is less than 4/5ths, or 80 percent, of the selection ratio for another protected group—are deemed to have disparate impact. Selection practices that have disparate impact are not considered unlawful if they are job-related or tied to a business necessity and no other reasonable alternatives with less disparate impact are available. Put another way, the selection practice is discriminatory if it shows disparate impact and the employer cannot provide sound evidence that it is job-related. Hiring procedures that are engineered to treat everyone the same, regardless of membership in a protected class, can prevent disparate impact. Relatedly, employers that regularly examine their selection procedures can better defend against claims of disparate impact.

One additional issue of legal defensibility concerns the potential for claims of what the media calls *reverse discrimination*. In a recent Supreme Court decision involving firefighters (*Ricci v. DeStephano*, 557 U.S. 557, 2009), the court clarified that selection decisions cannot be thrown out simply because there appeared to be disparate impact of the procedure. In that case, the employer chose to not examine whether the test was in fact valid. By not examining validity, the act of throwing out the decisions was determined to be unlawful because it was racially motivated (it was done specifically to increase minority representation). The case clarifies that employers cannot take actions to remedy or avoid unintentional disparate impact unless they have amassed certain types of evidence showing the practice would be considered unlawful under Title VII (see Biddle and Biddle, 2013, for more on this). Put simply, the *Ricci* case clarifies that changing a selection practice with the goal of increasing diversity may not be legally defensible.

Logistics and Timing

Efficient timing of selection procedures and their appropriate phasing in the process are additional factors to consider. For example, interviews, field investigations, medical examinations, and psychological examinations are too labor-intensive and cost-prohibitive to administer early in the selection process, when the candidate pool is at its peak. Alternatively, if written testing is administered early in the process, the large number of applicants requires a large-capacity locale for test administration and sufficient planning to allow candidates to schedule examinations without overwhelming the testing centers.

Difficulties in gathering enough staff for panel reviews, interviews, and written exams can also lead to scheduling problems that can excessively lengthen the selection process. For example, during the last cycle, the Personnel Department spent seven weeks conducting PIQ interviews, partly because staff could commit to running sessions only one day of the week.

Other issues—including that CPAT scores are only valid for a specified time period—can further impact how the selection process should be sequenced and timed. These types of logistic issues need to be carefully addressed.

Civil Service Standards, Guidelines, and Regulations

The Personnel Department and the LAFD must ensure that the selection process adheres to a series of regulations, policies, and procedures outlining scoring procedures, testing procedures, and the types of questions that can be asked. The Civil Service Rules and the City Charter impose explicit regulations on how tests are scored and candidates are certified. The Civil Service Rules and the City Charter dictate that candidates should be eligible for certification only if they score in the top "three whole scores" (City of Los Angeles Civil Service Rules, Section 5.8; City of Los Angeles Charter, Section 1010). To calculate this, a candidate's score on any "weighted"[6] (not pass/fail) test is averaged and then rounded to the nearest integer to provide their "whole score." Currently, the firefighter selection process has only one element that is weighted, the interview. This means that a candidate's final weighted score is simply his or her score on the interview. Candidates must therefore score 95, 100, or 105 (the top three possible scores) in order to move on and be certified. (Only candidates with military experience can achieve the highest score because the City Charter also mandates awarding a 5 percent credit for military service [City of Los Angeles

---

[6] This is the term used in the Civil Service Rules. We use it here to refer to the Civil Service's interpretation of the term only.

Charter, Section 1006].) If there are not enough candidates with the top three whole scores, the city can certify candidates further down the list until there are five more certified candidates than there are openings. All of the other selection steps except the interviews are treated as pass/fail, thus avoiding the "three whole scores" requirement. Civil Service Rules also dictate that the minimum passing score for a weighted written test is 65 percent.

A wide range of additional regulations and standards restrict how the LAFD and the Personnel Department conduct the selection process. Because firefighters are not sworn peace officers, the Personnel Department is limited in the questions they can ask candidates. For example, while a police officer candidate can be asked about prior arrest records, firefighter candidates can be asked only if they have actually been convicted of a crime. Background investigators are given POST (Peace Officer Standards and Training) training and abide by those rules when investigating firefighter candidates. The Americans with Disabilities Act and the Health Insurance Portability and Accountability Act (HIPAA) govern the amount of information that can be shared about the medical and psychological exams. Because of these two laws, the LAFD and the Personnel Department are prohibited from knowing why candidates were disqualified by these exams.

At most stages, candidates who are not chosen to move on in the process are not *disqualified*, but instead are issued a *non-select letter*. A disqualification means that a candidate cannot continue in the process but has a right to appeal the decision. Any process that disqualifies personnel typically leads to many appeals and an added resource burden on the Personnel Department. Not only can candidates appeal a *disqualification,* but they also have a chance to appeal a *non-select* decision after receiving their final score on the written test, or after the oral interview if they believe the interviewer made a mistake.

Defining Critical Firefighter Tasks, Knowledge, Skills, Abilities, and Other Characteristics

A job analysis is a systematic examination of the tasks or activities that individuals perform as part of their job, including the knowledge, skills, abilities, and other characteristics (KSAOs) needed to be successful in the job (Brannick, Levine, and Morgeson, 2007). Information from a job analysis serves as the foundation for many different aspects of personnel management, including the development of an effective selection system.[1] By helping identify the individual characteristics or attributes that are most likely to predict success on the job, an organization can then design a selection system that assesses the extent to which job candidates possess those specific attributes. Job analysis information is also critical from a legal defensibility standpoint if selection practices are challenged in court, because such information can enable an employer to demonstrate that a particular test or assessment method does not unlawfully discriminate on the basis of race, color, religion, sex, and national origin. For example, if a test or assessment method results in a protected group being hired at a significantly lower rate, such as fewer women being selected relative to men, the employer must be able to provide evidence that the test or assessment method is job-related.

---

[1] For more information see Society for Industrial and Organizational Psychology, Inc., 2003.

Existing LAFD Job Analyses

Because the 1994 and 2010 job analyses were so thorough, we believe that there is a solid foundation already in place with which to develop a sound selection system for LAFD firefighters. The 1994 job analysis study focused on identifying all tasks performed by firefighters assigned to engine companies and task forces, including basic firefighter competencies or knowledge, skills, and abilities that recruits need to possess. Based on this 1994 job analysis, the Personnel Department hired a private-sector firm to conduct a more detailed and updated job analysis in 2010. In the 2010 job analysis, researchers convened a panel of subject-matter experts consisting of battalion chiefs and fire captains, who reviewed and confirmed, with minor exceptions, the tasks and competencies already outlined in the 1994 report. The researchers then conducted a survey of a broader sample of subject-matter experts to establish the tasks and competencies most important on the job, including those most needed at the start of the job. Following the survey, additional subject-matter expert participation helped to further assess which competencies were needed to perform which tasks.

Overall, the job analysis identified 18 different overarching job duties (each with separate subtasks), ranging from ladder operations and sizing up a fire scene to emergency response and community relations. The analysis also identified eight overarching groups of competencies (each with separate subcompetencies) that were required to varying degrees to perform each of the job duties. These competency groups ranged from more general cognitive abilities and thinking and reasoning skills to written and oral communication, interpersonal skills, and physical abilities.

Supplementing the Existing Job Analyses

The RAND study team sought to determine whether the 1994 job analysis and its 2010 update still accurately captured what firefighters do in their job and to identify potential gaps or areas that require updating to more accurately reflect what the job currently entails and the competencies that should be assessed as part of the selection system. We accomplished this by (1) reviewing a broad range of literature on firefighter job requirements, including online firefighter job descriptions from a variety of fire departments nationwide and the Occupational Information Network (O*NET),[2] and (2) conducting focus group interviews at three fire stations in geographically and demographically distinct locations throughout Los Angeles. Fifteen firefighters and three fire captains were interviewed, for a total of 18. Firefighters were asked to write down their initial thoughts on what makes an effective/ineffective firefighter. They were also asked to review (1) a detailed list of 73 firefighter duty tasks that were grouped into 18 categories and (2) a list of 58 competencies, all of which were outlined in the 2010 job analysis report. In a separate interview, we gave the same instructions to the fire captains.

For the most part, focus group participants felt that the list of duty tasks identified in the 2010 job analysis report accurately reflects their current responsibilities. Relatedly, the majority of the firefighter competencies that were described as essential in the 2010 job analysis were confirmed during our interviews, with many being labeled as more critical now compared with past years. Table B.1 shows competencies that were mentioned in the 2010 report and reemphasized during our focus groups, and Table B.2 provides the full list of comments and suggestions made by focus group participants on how to expand the list of firefighter duty tasks.

---

[2]   O*NET, an online resource provided by the U.S. Department of Labor Employment and Training Administration, provides a database that contains information on hundreds of standardized and occupation-specific descriptors. The database is continually updated by surveying a broad range of workers from each occupation.

Table B.1
Competencies Documented in 2010 and Reinforced in RAND Focus Groups

Validated Firefighter Competencies

- Mechanical aptitude
- Decisive decisionmaking
- Physical and mental stamina
- Patience
- Empathy
- Initiative
- Self-discipline
- Problem-solving skills
- A positive public demeanor
- The ability to work in teams yet avoid groupthink
- A sense of humor
- The ability to accept constructive criticism

Suggested New Firefighter Competencies

- The ability to deal with the threat posed by people's pets and the ability to show compassion toward people's pets
- Being comfortable with uncertainty
- The ability to leverage prior work and life experience
- Mental resiliency/courage to seek support when coping with the difficult demands of the job
- Computer skills

Table B.2
Suggestions for Expanding the List of Firefighter Duty Tasks

Lifts and Carries the Following Equipment WITHOUT Assistance

- All three focus groups suggested adding the "jaws of life."
- One focus group mentioned adding the equipment for vertical ventilation, which includes *simultaneously* carrying chains and a sprinkler kit (80 lbs.), a 45-lb. breather, and a 15-lb. heart monitor (LifePak).
- On a related point, the focus group thought it was important to note that firefighters are often carrying heavy equipment while simultaneously wearing heavy gear.
- The same focus group suggested deleting the duty task of carrying fittings, couplings, and nozzles, most of which are not very heavy, except for the four-way fitting (~40 lbs.).
- Cribbing and gurneys were additional items mentioned by another focus group.

Lifts and Carries the Following WITH Assistance

- One focus group suggested adding the rescue air cushion (not all trucks have it but it requires 6 people to carry). The same group also wanted to add the litter basket, which can be used to rescue a person or haul equipment. The group also suggested removing the portable extinguisher from this list, which, at 60 lbs. or less, firefighters are expected to carry on their own.
- All three focus groups noted that victims can weigh in excess of 450 lbs. One firefighter mentioned that the 450-lb. limit might have been derived from the weight restrictions for a standard gurney, though patients can easily weigh more than that.

Emergency Response

- One focus group felt it was important to reiterate the importance of driving to locations in a safe manner. It may be beneficial to reword Duty Task No. 13 to read, "Select the best route to the emergency site and "safely" drive apparatus or ambulance to the site of emergency using warning lights and siren, as needed, in all kinds of weather and traffic."

Sizes Up Fire Scene

- One focus group felt it would be a good idea to add a task for "Forcible Entry," which entails one firefighter dedicated to determining where and how best to enter a structure using the appropriate tools and techniques.

Table B.2—Continued

Enters Fire Structures

- One focus group noted that No. 17 on the original list is inaccurate—people entering the building do not determine if ventilation is needed. Vertical ventilation is a separate task and one that all three focus groups felt merits its own duty task heading. One focus group suggested also adding horizontal ventilation to the list.
- A "vertical ventilation" task description would entail a team of firefighters capable of moving to the roof of a structure, identifying and understanding the roof construction, sounding the roof with a rubbish hook for structural integrity. A lead firefighter then operates the chainsaw, before additional firefighters pull materials out and/or punch the ceiling in to give the engine company relief. Firefighters must have a good understanding of the vocabulary of roof ventilation operations (what is a "pull back" or a "strip") to cut a hole to clear the smoke and heated gases. They must also be prepared to listen to the radio, take in the changing conditions on the roof, and communicate changing conditions to the chief/engine.

Carries Out Ladder Operations

No issues reported.

Performs Hose and Extinguisher Operations

- One focus group noted that it was important to describe smoke and visibility issues that may arise while conducting hose and extinguishing operations. Additionally, firefighters sometimes have to use a 2.5-in. hose line without assistance—they use a strap to tie it off, loop it, sit on it, or stand there and hold it.
- One focus group suggested adding the dropping and retracting of a drop bag, a 20–100 lbs. 1.75-in. (sometimes 2.5-in.) line that firefighters carry to the top of a multistory building.

Makes Readings, Estimates, and Calculations

- One focus group suggested adding aerial ladder specifications: Firefighters need to understand and apply the load chart that determines the capacity maximum of the ladder depending on its angle and extension.

Protects People and Property

- All three focus groups suggested adding "exposure protection," or preventing the spread of the fire by hosing down uninvolved structures, cutting down trees, covering attic vents, etc.
- One focus group suggested adding "cordoning off the area to protect people and lessen unnecessary distractions from crisis response efforts."
- Two focus groups recommended adding "protection of the crew" to this duty task section.

Table B.2—Continued

Participates in Rescue Operations

- There was consensus among all three fire stations that the 450-lb. weight limit for carrying patients with assistance is too low. All three stations have witnessed patients easily exceeding that limit. Weight can vary so much it may not be useful to include an exact limit at all.
- One focus group wanted to add wall breaching to access victims and downed firefighters.
- One focus group mentioned the importance of making difficult decisions regarding victim prioritization, assessing whom to take, what order to attend to them in, and the possibility that deceased victims might have to be left behind.
- One focus group noted that firefighters have to coordinate and communicate with the Los Angeles Police Department and a host of other city agencies and departments (i.e., Drinking Water Program, Department of Health Services, Hazardous Materials Response Team (HAZMAT), L.A. County Animal Care and Control).

Participates in Salvage, Overhaul, and Cleanup Operations

- Two focus groups took issue with the weight limits as described in the original report. One focus group felt 100 lbs. is probably too low of a weight limit for objects firefighters are expected to carry without assistance during salvage, overhaul, and cleanup operations, suggesting that 150 lbs. is closer to reality. The other focus group felt that once extinguished, the weight of a burnt mattress, for example, will exceed 100 lbs. and would likely require assistance by at least one other firefighter.

Performs Emergency Medical Treatment

- Two focus groups suggested including computer-related tasks associated with documenting and reporting patient care.
- The suburban focus group added that firefighters must also know how to assess psychiatric patients.
- All three focus groups suggested adding transferring patients to hospitals when necessary. This includes coordinating with hospital staff, handing over documentation, and waiting with the patient until a bed becomes available.

Participates in Dealing with Hazardous Materials Incidents

- All three focus groups felt the current description of HAZMAT removal was misleading. One focus group asserted that firefighters do not remove hazardous materials. Another said HAZMAT situations are reserved for certified personnel on specialized task forces more than the general firefighter. The last focus group felt firefighters might remove some hazardous materials such as fuel cans, but higher-risk materials would be left to the appropriate city, state, federal, and other agencies. Further clarification of HAZMAT removal responsibilities might be in order.

Table B.2—Continued

Participates in Fire Prevention, Inspections, and Public Safety

- All three focus groups felt this section omitted an important task associated with fire inspections: the opportunity for firefighters to take mental notes on a specific structure to better prepare them in the event that an emergency occurs at that location.

Performs Station Maintenance and Maintains Cooperative Relationships with Department Staff

No issues reported.

Maintains Apparatus and Equipment

- One focus group added that apparatus and equipment maintenance also includes running diagnostics on tools, calling in repairs, and coordinating repairs with mechanic shops.
- Another focus group felt the list was misleading and might be interpreted as exhaustive when the actual amount of equipment to maintain far exceeds this list. The group suggested a more general description that is more all-encompassing rather than trying to capture all maintenance responsibilities in detail.

Community Relations

- One participant from a focus group mentioned adding the Cadet Program to this task. Of note, this participant was the Cadet Program leader at this fire station and the only focus group to have one present during the focus group. No one else from any focus group mentioned this as a key task, which might suggest firefighters who are not involved in this voluntary post deem this as of lesser importance and overly time-consuming considering the other critical and demanding job expectations.
- All three focus groups felt it was important to remind firefighters that as public servants, community relations are an ongoing responsibility that occurs both on and off the job.

Participates in Training and Professional Development

- One focus group suggested not only attending training/development activities, but teaching them as well. "Everyone is responsible for mentoring rookies."

Outsourcing the Written Test for Entry-Level Firefighters

Although the current written aptitude test to select LAFD firefighters is developed in-house, outsourcing the test and its administration to a vendor can have several advantages (e.g., the test would be developed by experts, the test would have support for test validity and reliability). Below, we provide information on selected vendors and their tests using a number of key criteria.

Alternative Written Aptitude Tests

Outsourcing the entry-level firefighter exam to a private vendor has a number of advantages over in-house test development. Private vendors commonly conduct validation studies to determine the efficacy of their tests. Additionally, private vendors that specialize in test making often use experienced professionals, such as industrial/organizational psychologists and subject-matter experts, to produce relevant test questions that can identify the best firefighters for the job.

To identify potential alternative aptitude tests, RAND contacted 17 fire departments[1] from heavily and moderately populated cities, in addition to personnel and human resources departments, and asked

---

[1] The following cities were contacted: District of Columbia, Boston, Chicago, Houston, Dallas, Topeka, Tulsa, Phoenix, Denver, Miami, New York City, Pittsburgh, Albuquerque, Tampa, Atlanta, Austin, Indianapolis.

whether they outsourced their entry-level firefighter exam[2] or produced it in-house. Of the 20 cities that were contacted, three produced it in-house, seven did not respond to our inquiries, and ten reported outsourcing the exam to private vendors. Of those ten cities using vendors, only five identified the vendors by name. In total, three vendors were identified: Ergometrics, CWH Management Solutions, and I/O Solutions, with some cities using the same vendor. The remaining five cities refrained from identifying to whom they outsourced their exam.

Below, we examine each of these three vendors and the written tests they provide, using the following criteria:

- Test content: the extent to which the test measures content relevant to the knowledge, skills, and abilities needed to be a firefighter
- Test development: the information and methods used to develop the test content, particularly, the extent to which the test was based on information from a job analysis
- Validity and reliability: the extent to which there is research evidence for the validity and reliability of the tests (i.e., the relationship between the test and important job performance criteria)
- Test administration: options for who administers the test and how it is administered
- The availability of different test versions: the number of different versions available of the test[3]
- Administration costs: cost to the Personnel Department and applicants for using/taking the test
- Availability of study material: the extent to which the vendor provides study material to help applicants prepare for the test.

---

[2]   This report only discusses the entry-level firefighter written exam and not the promotional written exam. RAND decided to focus solely on the entry-level exam due to the high volume turnout during the two days of testing and the controversial nature of the test results.

[3]   No specific number of versions is needed; however, the existence of multiple versions allows for retesting and ensures test security to prevent cheating from one administration to the next. The more versions available, the more secure the test content and the more chances for retesting.

These criteria are not exhaustive, but we view them as being the most critical factors to consider when selecting a test, with the validity and reliability of the test being the most important. Note that our review focuses on only the three alternative tests we were able to identify in our search; note also that some variation exists in the depth of information we were able to identify in our search, as well as in the depth of information we were able to obtain for each vendor. Therefore, this effort should be viewed as only a preliminary step in a larger effort to provide implementable alternatives to the written exam. Tables C.1 through C.3 summarize our findings on the three vendors (Ergometrics, CWH Management Solutions, and I/O Solutions).

Although we describe these three vendors for purposes of illustrating some of the testing options that are available, these three vendors are not the only qualified organizations to consider. For example, Fire & Police Selection, Inc., is another organization that provides a variety of selection tests for firefighters and should be considered as well.[4]

---

[4]   For more on FPSI's selection tests see http://www.fpsi.com/matrix.html.

Table C.1
Ergometrics

Additional Information: The test is called the FireTEAM Testing System and is administered by the National Testing Network (NTN).	
Test components	• Primary content includes reading, arithmetic, mechanical reasoning, and a human relations video test. • Ergometrics also provides dimensional scores on the following candidate tendencies: abrasiveness, causes tension, authoritarian, inconsiderate, low tolerance, passive, self-focused, work avoidance, supervisor relations.
Test development	• Industrial/organizational psychologists and fire department subject-matter experts developed the test. The dimensions are provided by the subject-matter experts and are designed to cover areas untouched in other training programs. Subject-matter experts must reach full consensus on material, answer choices, and their respective weighting.
Validity and reliability	• Ergometrics ensures that its current FireTEAM Testing System conforms to legal and professional standards for test validation, including those established by the Equal Employment Opportunity Commission and the Office of Federal Contract Compliance. • Over 310 firefighters from four different cities were included in a validity study. Firefighters with three months' to five years' experience were selected to participate. • Over 300 firefighters from six different cities and counties completed a written job analysis survey, quantifying and verifying the contributions of expert panels that worked on the test content. • An analysis of over 8,000 applicant cases confirmed that the FireTEAM Testing System has less disparate impact than traditional written cognitive ability tests.
Test administration	• The test is a series of approximately 78 video simulations, each with four answer choices. Test takers are given ten seconds to provide the best solution to a situation. Answers are weighted. • Fire departments can either lease the test and administer themselves or use National Testing Network centers, which conduct the proctoring, scheduling, and tracking of candidates. Leasing the exam can result in more barriers for candidates, according to information provided to Ergometrics from various fire departments. • There are four testing centers in Southern California, with another forthcoming. Candidates schedule tests at their convenience. Testing is done continually.
Alternate test versions	• None.
Administration costs	• For $2,500 per year, NTN handles all aspects of the test administration; candidates then pay NTN $40 to take the exam and/or $7 to have their scores transferred to other fire departments. There is a hardship, or voucher, program for those who cannot pay.
Availability of study materials	• Free practice tests are available.

**Table C.2
CWH Management Solutions**

Additional Information: The test is called the Next Generation Written Test.	
Test components	• Primary content includes reading comprehension, arithmetic, mechanical reasoning. • Secondary content includes practical skills, interpersonal skills, and emotional outlook.
Test development	• To develop the Next Generation Written Test, CWH conducted a job analysis in partnership with several fire departments from different regions of the country in order to define the firefighter position on a national level. • 84 job experts from 30 different departments reviewed a job analysis questionnaire to ensure that it covered the full range of firefighter and EMT/paramedic job duties and KSAOs. It was then administered to 1,231 fire service/EMT personnel from 18 different departments. The test was then designed to assess the skills and abilities that were rated by respondents as being the most critical and important to the entry-level firefighter/EMT position.
Validity and reliability	• A validation study conducted by CWH found that the composite test score from the Next Generation test predicted firefighter job performance with an uncorrected correlation of 0.35. Relatedly, the validity coefficient was 0.29 for the firefighter job performance when using the Supervisor Performance Rating as the criterion. By industry standards, these uncorrected correlation coefficients speak very favorably to the validity of the test. These correlations support the assertion that people who do better on the test are better job performers. • CWH provides both incumbent *and* actual applicant data for the test. Using actual applicant data allows CWH to provide a more realistic depiction of disparate impact results to a firefighter candidate pool.
Test administration	• The test is a paper-and-pencil format and is typically administered by the client (i.e., a fire department). CWH customarily handles the scoring of the exam, for which it uses statistical software.
Alternate test versions	• Two different test versions are available.
Administration costs	• Applicant test materials; scoring and analysis typically costs $14 per person, with a minimum of $210; the setup fee for the first test administration (one-time annual fee) is $300; applicant feedback reports are $0.50 per person, with a minimum of $125.
Availability of study materials	• A study guide is sold for $1.50 (price per study guide, sold in pack of 50) to help applicants prepare for the written test. The guide does not contain memorization information and instead familiarizes applicants with the content and format of the test.

Table C.3
I/O Solutions

Additional Information: The test is called the National Firefighter Selection Inventory (NFSI) compensatory examination tool.

Test components	• Primary content includes reading comprehension, mathematical reasoning, deductive reasoning, and sensitivity and spatial orientation. • I/O Solutions' NFSI is based on an industrial psychology approach to assess emotional outlook, behavioral predispositions, and situational awareness, in addition to basic math/English skills (no mechanical aptitude testing).
Test development	• The exam was based on extensive job analyses conducted on entry-level positions throughout the nation; additionally, I/O Solutions reviewed past job analyses from fire departments in 13 different states. • The job analysis entailed (1) experienced job analysts spending several days observing and noting employees' actual behaviors, the equipment used, and the tasks performed; and (2) interviews with a sample of job incumbents that elicited the workers' perceptions of what they do on the job and why. • In creating the NFSI, I/O Solutions used the data gleaned from their observations and job incumbent interviews to create four separate lists that detailed the personality, psychological, physical, and cognitive requirements for the firefighter job.
Validity and reliability	• Several U.S. cities conducted criterion validation studies on the NFSI. • A validity *generalization* study was conducted for the NFSI using two criteria. The first criterion looked at the relationship between the NFSI and academic performance; the second assessed the relationship between the NFSI and on-the-job performance. Both investigations used data gathered from multiple smaller validation studies on the NFSI.
Test administration	• The test is administered using either a paper-and-pencil or online. I/O Solutions also has a web-based platform (PS3) it can make accessible to departments; scores from the PS3 are immediately available. • Fire departments can also become certified test administrators and proctor the NFSI themselves.
Alternate test versions	• Five different test versions are available.
Administration costs	• Applicant test materials; scoring and analysis typically costs $18 per person; no setup fee or minimum order required.
Availability of study materials	• Candidates can purchase a study guide for $6.95 and fire departments can purchase the same study guide for $4.00, with no minimum order required.

The Impact of Chance Variability in Simple Random Sampling

In Chapter Five, we discussed the possibility of using a random selection process as a cost- and time-saving method for reducing the number of applicants to process. However, one such method—a simple random sample—has some disadvantages, because chance alone will likely result in a sample that does not exactly match the demographic profile of the pool of people from which the sample was drawn. This appendix illustrates how much the demographic profile of a simple random sample can be expected to vary.

Overview of the Reasoning for Selecting a Random Sample

Historically, a much larger number of applicants take and pass the written test than can be admitted to the next phase of the process. One option for selecting candidates from among those who passed their written test is to draw a simple random sample from the qualified pool of applicants. The size of the sample would be determined to coincide with a reasonable number that the system can accommodate. The diversity of the sample would reflect the diversity of the pool of applicants. That is, the expected proportion of such a sample that is non-Hispanic white and the expected proportion that is male are each equal to the respective proportions in the qualified pool of applicants.[1] Suppose a given qualified pool of applicants is 50 percent white,[2] and a large number of random samples are drawn from the applicant pool; the average percentage of whites across all the samples would be approximately 50 percent. However, the percentage of whites in any one individual random sample may naturally deviate from 50 percent, and, of course, only a single sample would be drawn when implementing a random sample to determine which qualified applicants move to the next phase. Below, we investigate how far we may expect individual random samples to deviate from the representative percentages of whites and males in the qualified applicant pool.

The 2013 applicant cohort taking and passing the written test was 50.34 percent white and 94.30 percent male. We use these as baseline percentages for a qualified applicant pool for a hypothetical future random sample, and consider random samples of qualified applicants ranging in size from 300 to 1,000. Figure D.1 displays a series of probability intervals for the proportion of whites in a random sample from an applicant pool that is 50.34 percent white. The blue lines on the graph represent an 80 percent probability interval for each sample size indicated on the horizontal axis; 80 percent of the time, the percentage of whites in a sample will fall between the upper and lower blue lines in the graph. Ten percent of the time, the percentage of whites in the sample will be above the upper blue line, and 10 percent of the time it will be below the lower blue line. For example, for a sample size of 300 (the leftmost endpoints on the graph), the 80 percent probability interval is [46.6%, 54.0%]. With an individual sample of size 300 from a pool that is 50.3 percent white, there is a 1-in-10 chance that white representation in the sample will exceed 54.0 percent, and, similarly, a 1-in-10 chance that the percentage of whites in the sample would fall below 46.6 percent. Figure D.1 also displays 50 percent (black line), 90 percent (green line), and 98 percent (red line) probability intervals.

---

[1]   In this section, we focus on the percentages of non-Hispanic white and males selected. However, the rationale presented applies to all races/ethnicities and both genders, and well as any other sub-group represented in the sample.

[2]   Throughout, "white" is intended to mean non-Hispanic white only.

Figure D.1
Probability Intervals for the Percentage of Whites in a Random Sample from an Applicant Pool That Is 50.34 Percent White

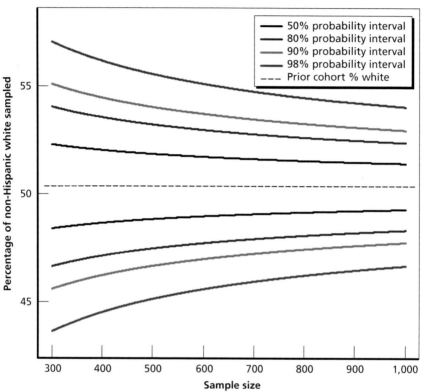

RAND *RR687-D.1*

White representation in a simple random sample from an applicant pool that is 50.3 percent white has a 1-in-4 chance of falling above the black line, a 1-in-20 chance of falling above the green line, and a 1-in-100 chance of falling above the red line, with a similar chance of falling below the lower line for each color. As seen in the graph, the width of the probability intervals shrinks as the sample size increases, implying that as sample size increases the chances of experiencing a sample that deviates from applicant pool representation by a particular amount get smaller. However, in sample sizes closer to 1,000, the rate of improvement is smaller than is seen in smaller sample sizes.

Figure D.2
Probability Intervals for the Percentage of Males in a Random Sample from an Applicant Pool That Is 94.30 Percent Male

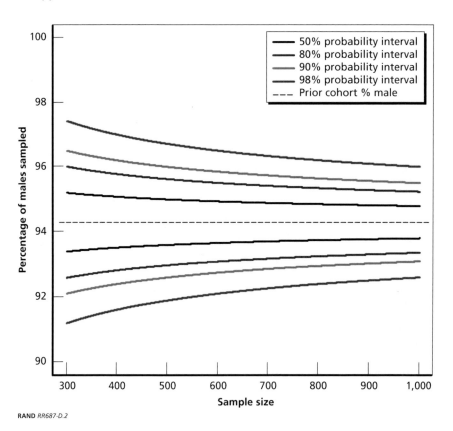

Across the full range of sample sizes examined (300 to 1,000), the chance of having white representation in the sample more than five percentage points above the representation of 50.34 percent in the applicant pool is always less than 1 in 20, and for sample sizes of 542 and above, that chance is less than 1 in 100. The same probabilities hold for deviations of five percentage points below applicant pool representation.

Figure D.2 presents analogous probability intervals for the percentage of males in a simple random sample from an applicant pool that is 94.30 percent male. Because the percentage of the applicant pool that is male is close to 100 percent, the probability intervals are smaller in this case.[3] Consequently, the chance of experiencing a male representation in the sample that deviates even three percentage points below applicant pool representation is less than 1 in 100 for sample sizes of 323 and above, with similar chances of a deviation of three percentage points above.

---

[3]   In general, such intervals would be largest when representation in the qualified applicant pool is 50 percent and become smaller as the representation moves away from 50 percent in either direction.

Mathematics and Examples of Key Considerations for Stratified Sampling

In this appendix, we describe the statistical approach known as stratified random sampling and the mathematics associated with it. For illustration purposes, we offer an example using a population similar to that involved in the firefighter context. However, there are many detailed nuances that are beyond the scope of this report, as any stratified sampling practice would need to be tailored to the exact population in question and the context and goals of that sampling would need to be clearly specified before sound direction could be given. Also, as we have noted in the preface and elsewhere, there are significant legal implications in handling race information in a selection context. We do not address those legal issues here, and we reiterate that any stratified process should be carefully reviewed by the city's legal counsel.

In Appendix D, we discussed the chance variability that can occur in the use of a simple random sample. We noted that with such a procedure all applicants would have an equal probability of selection; however, the proportion of a subgroup of interest represented in the applicant pool and in a simple random sample would naturally differ because of sampling variability. For example, in Figure D.1, we saw that when drawing a simple random sample of size 300 from an applicant pool that is 50 percent white, the resulting percentage of white applicants in the selected sample would fall between 45 and 55 percent approximately 90 percent of the time.

Stratified random sampling is an alternative sampling method in which the sample is independently drawn from mutually exclusive subgroups[1] of interest (i.e., *strata*) within the group of people from which the sample is being drawn (i.e., the *sampling frame*),[2] thereby allowing the sampling properties of the subgroups to be refined. Stratification may be used as a feature of a sampling design to ensure the representation of properly defined subgroups within the sampling frame (Groves et al., 2004). In particular, *proportional allocation to strata* is a technique by which the sample is selected within each stratum with the same probability of selection (Groves et al., 2004), so that each member of the sampling frame has the same probability of being selected into the sample and each well-defined stratum is represented in the sample at the same rate at which it appears in the sampling frame. In this context, if all applicants were properly classified into the correct subgroups, proportional allocation would enable us to draw a stratified sample in which all subgroups of interest were represented proportionally to their presence in the applicant pool. For example, when using proportional allocation to draw a random sample stratified by race/ethnicity from an applicant pool that is 50 percent white, the resulting sample would also be 50 percent white.[3]

Stratified Sampling Formulas Illustrated with an Example

Suppose the sampling frame (or the group from which people will be sampled) consists of 10,000 members, each of which belongs to one of three strata, such that 60 percent of the frame is in stratum A, 10 percent is in stratum B, and the remaining 30 percent is in stratum C. Table E.1 illustrates the resultant size of each stratum in the second

---

[1]   Such groups are mutually exclusive if each member of the sampling frame belongs to one and only one of the groups.

[2]   Note that in the case of drawing a stratified random sample of job applicants, for example, the sampling frame would differ depending on when in the selection process the stratified sampling was taking place.

[3]   Depending on that sample size, the exact proportion of the sample may not match the exact proportion of the sampling frame. In the example, a sample size of 301 could not yield a sample with 150.5 white applicants. See the section on additional considerations below for further discussion.

Table E.1
Stratified Sampling Example, In Which 3 Percent of Each Sub-Population Is Selected

Strata	Number in Sampling Frame	Proportion of Sampling Frame	Number in Sample	Proportion of Sample	Probability of Selection
A	6,000	0.6	180	0.6	$\frac{180}{6,000} = 0.03$
B	1,000	0.1	30	0.1	$\frac{30}{1,000} = 0.03$
C	3,000	0.3	90	0.3	$\frac{90}{3,000} = 0.03$
Total	10,000	1.0	300	1.0	0.03

column. The third column shows the proportion that the number of people in each stratum represents within the sampling frame (e.g., there are 6,000 people in stratum A and 10,000 people in the sampling frame; 6,000/10,000 = 0.6 or 60 percent).

Now suppose that we have chosen to randomly select 3 percent of the people from each stratum (i.e., everyone in the stratum has a 0.03 probability of being selected), as shown in the far right column. Column 4 shows how many people need to be randomly sampled from each stratum to achieve the 0.03 probability of selection (e.g., 6,000 × 0.03 = 180, so 180 need to be selected from stratum A). Column 5 shows the proportion of the resulting sample from each stratum relative to the total number of people selected (e.g., out of the total sample of 300, 180 people [or 60 percent] will be members of stratum A; 180/300 = 0.6 or 60 percent). Note that the proportion of the sampling frame matches the proportion of the sample in the example. This example illustrates one type of stratified sampling: *stratified random sampling using proportional allocation to strata.*

We now detail the mathematics for this type of stratified sample. The sampling frame consists of N people, each of whom is a member of one of G well-defined, mutually exclusive subgroups of interest (strata), indexed by $g \in \{1,...,G\}$. Let N_g represent the size of stratum g in the sampling frame. Since the strata are mutually exclusive, the individual strata sizes sum to N, i.e., $\sum_{g=1}^{G} N_g = N$, and each stratum represents $\frac{N_g}{N}$ of the total sampling frame. Further, suppose that a sample of size n from the sampling frame is desired, such that each stratum represents $\frac{N_g}{N}$ of the total sample; i.e., the proportion of each stratum in the sample matches the proportion of each stratum in the sampling frame. The sample is generated by drawing a simple random sample from each stratum of size $n_g = \frac{n \cdot N_g}{N_g}$, with each member of stratum g having probability $\frac{n_g}{N_g}$ of being sampled. For the moment, we assume $n_g = \frac{n \cdot N_g}{N_g}$ is an integer; see the additional considerations section below for the non-integer case. This sample includes the following features:

1. The samples from each stratum sum to produce the desired overall sample size n:

$$\sum_{g=1}^{G} n_g = \sum_{g=1}^{G} \frac{n \cdot N_g}{N} = \frac{n}{N} \sum_{g=1}^{G} N_g = n.$$

2. The proportion of stratum g found in the sample matches the proportion of stratum g found in the sampling frame:

$$\frac{n_g}{n} = \frac{1}{n} \cdot \frac{n \cdot N_g}{N} = \frac{N_g}{N}.$$

3. Each member of the sampling frame has an equal probability of selection, regardless of the stratum to which they belong:

$$P(\text{person } i \text{ selected} \mid \text{member of stratum } g) = \frac{n_g}{N_g} = \frac{1}{N_g} \cdot \frac{n \cdot N_g}{N} = \frac{n}{N}.$$

While the simple random sample approach would also produce a sample of size n, with each member of the sampling frame having an equal probability of selection, this stratified random sampling approach also yields a sample distribution of the strata equivalent to that distribution in the sampling frame (feature 2 above).

Additional Considerations

In the context of using stratified random sampling with proportional allocation where strata are defined and samples are drawn using someone's self-reported race or ethnicity, several additional considerations are worth noting.[4] One is what to do when not all of the calculated strata sample sizes n_g are integers, as will likely be the case. For example, suppose in the example in Table E.1., the strata sizes in the sampling frame were instead 5,860 for stratum A, 1,095 for stratum B, and 3,045 for stratum C, with corresponding strata sample sizes of 175.80, 32.85, and 91.35. This poses a dilemma, because it is impossible to select 175.80 people. A reasonable approach is to round down the strata sample sizes to the next lowest integer, with the remaining selections attributed randomly to the strata, proportional to the fraction lost by the rounding. In this example, rounding down yields integer sample sizes of 175, 32, and 91, for a total of 298, with two selections left to allocate. Each of the remaining two selections would be randomly allocated to strata A, B, and C with probabilities 0.400, 0.425, and 0.175, respectively. The probabilities are determined by dividing the remaining fraction after rounding by the number left to allocate.[5] Such an allocation procedure would preserve the characteristic that everyone in the sampling frame has an equal probability of selection (feature 3 above). Feature 2 would be retained approximately, with a small sampling error.[6]

Another consideration for implementing stratified random sampling is the necessity for properly defined mutually exclusive groupings determining the strata. In the context of the applicant pool, this requirement may not be met, for several reasons. First, when using

---

[4] These are some examples of those potential concerns, but they are not an exhaustive list.

[5] For example, stratum B had a calculated sample size of 32.85; rounding down to an allocation of 32 left a remaining fraction of 0.85. Diving 0.85 by 2 remaining allocations gives 0.425 to use as the allocation probability.

[6] An alternative strategy here would be to randomly assign the first of the two remaining allocations among the three strata using these probabilities, and then assign the final allocation to one of the other two not chosen, rescaling their respective probabilities to sum to one. Feature 2 (approximately) and feature 3 would again be retained.

race/ethnicity as strata, some applicants may belong to multiple racial ethnic groups. For example, an applicant may be both black and Hispanic. If a category of black Hispanic is not offered when racial/ethnic data are collected, such applicants would be placed into whichever of these two strata to which they self-identify for the purpose of sampling; however, sampling such an applicant would increase the numbers of both blacks and Hispanics sampled.

Second, applicants may decline to provide racial/ethnic data, leaving them without a stratum. One solution for this case would be to create an additional "declined" stratum to be treated as any other in the stratified sampling process. Feature 2 would still technically hold given the definition of this new stratum; in practical terms, the racial/ethnic distribution among non-decliners in the applicant pool would still match the racial/ethnic distribution among non-decliners in the resulting sample, while the racial/ethnic distribution among decliners in the applicant pool and in the sample would naturally differ due to sampling variability.[7]

Third, the requirement to have properly defined racial/ethnic strata may not be met because self-reporting of this information allows for potential misreporting. Such misclassification would *not* alter the probability of selection for any individual in the applicant pool, including those misclassified. However, in the presence of misclassification, the reason for conducting stratified random sampling instead of taking a simple random sample (i.e., the goal of ensuring that distribution of race/ethnicity in the sample does not deviate from the distribution in the sampling frame because of chance alone, as would be the case for simple random sampling explained in Appendix D) would not be fully achieved. Although the reported distributions of race/ethnicity in the applicant pool and the sample would still match, the strata into which applicants are misclassified would actually contain applicants of multiple races/ethnicities due to the misclassification, introducing sampling variability into the number of applicants actually chosen from each race/ethnicity in each of those strata. The practical significance of the

---

[7]   Luck of the draw could technically produce a match, but this is highly unlikely in all but the most trivial of cases.

introduction of variability in the number of applicants actually sampled from each race/ethnicity depends on the amount of the misclassification. As misclassification grows, the chances for larger deviations between the desired number sampled from each race/ethnicity and the actual number sampled increase, although such deviations are equally likely to be positive or negative (as seen in Appendix D).

A final example consideration is what size sample is needed overall, which in turn sets the desired proportion that should be sampled from each of the groups. In the illustration offered above, we set the proportion at 0.03, or 3 percent. In actuality, that proportion might be driven by any number of considerations, such as the desired minimum number of people needed in the smallest stratum, the maximum number needed in the largest stratum, or the total desired in the overall sample.

References

American Educational Research Association, American Psychological Association, National Council on Measurement in Education, and Joint Committee on Standards for Educational and Psychological Testing, *Standards for Educational and Psychological Testing*, 2014.

Asch, Beth J., and Bruce R. Orvis, *Recent Recruiting Trends and Their Implications: Preliminary Analysis and Recommendations,* Santa Monica, Calif.: RAND Corporation, MR-549-A/OSD, 1994. As of July 3, 2014:
http://www.rand.org/pubs/monograph_reports/MR549.html

Barrett, Gerald V., Michael D. Polomsky, and Michael A. Daniel, "Selection Tests for Firefighters: A Comprehensive Review and Meta-Analysis," *Journal of Business and Psychology*, Vol. 13, No. 4, 1999, pp. 507–513.

Barrick, Murray R., and Michael K. Mount, "The Big Five Personality Dimensions and Job Performance: A Meta-Analysis," *Personnel Psychology*, Vol. 44, No. 1, 1991, pp. 1–26.

Biddle, Richard E., and Daniel A. Biddle, "What Public-Sector Employers Need to Know About Promotional Practices, Procedures, and Tests in Public Safety Promotional Processes After *Ricci v. DeStefano*," *Public Personnel Management*, Vol. 42, No. 2, 2013, pp. 151–190.

Brannick, Michael T., Edward L. Levine, and Frederick P. Morgeson, *Job and Work Analysis: Methods, Research, and Applications for Human Resource Management*, Thousand Oaks, Calif.: Sage Publications, 2007.

Burkhauser, Susan, Lawrence M. Hanser, and Chaitra M. Hardison, *Elements of Success: How Type of Secondary Education Credential Helps Predict Enlistee Attrition*, Santa Monica, Calif.: RAND Corporation, RR-374-OSD, 2014. As of November 17, 2014:
http://www.rand.org/pubs/research_reports/RR374.html

California Fire Fighter Joint Apprenticeship Committee, *CPAT (Candidate Physical Ability Test): Candidate Preparation Guide*, 2007. As of November 17, 2014:
http://www.cffjac.org/go/
jac/?LinkServID=3E94B79A-1CC4-C201-3E4BF872E67CB568

Campion, Michael A. "Personnel Selection for Physically Demanding Jobs: Review and Recommendations," *Personnel Psychology*, Vol. 36, No. 3, 1983, pp. 527–550.

Chapman, Derek S., Krista L. Uggerslev, Sarah A. Carroll, Kelly A. Piasentin, and David A. Jones, "Applicant Attraction to Organizations and Job Choice: A Meta-Analytic Review of the Correlates of Recruiting Outcomes," *Journal of Applied Psychology*, Vol. 90, No. 5, 2005, p. 928.

City of Los Angeles Charter. As of July 28, 2014:
http://lacity.org/government/CityCharterRulesandCodes/index.htm

City of Los Angeles, Civil Service Rules (*Rules of the Board of Civil Service Commissioners*), August 2012. As of July 28, 2014:
http://per.lacity.org/pdf/csvcrules.pdf

Colquitt, Jason A., Donald E. Conlon, Michael J. Wesson, Christopher O. L. H. Porter, and K. Yee Ng, "Justice at the Millennium: A Meta-Analytic Review of 25 Years of Organizational Justice Research," *Journal of Applied Psychology*, Vol. 86, No. 3, 2001, p. 425.

Cullen, Michael J., Chaitra M. Hardison, and Paul R. Sackett, "Using SAT-Grade and Ability-Job Performance Relationships to Test Predictions Derived from Stereotype Threat Theory," *Journal of Applied Psychology*, Vol. 89, April 2004, pp. 220–230.

De Soete, Britt, Filip Lievens, and Celina Druart, "Strategies for Dealing with the Diversity-Validity Dilemma in Personnel Selection: Where Are We and Where Should We Go?" *Journal of Work and Organizational Psychology*, Vol. 29, 2013, pp. 3–12.

Equal Employment Opportunity Commission, "Uniform Guidelines on Employee Selection Procedures," *Federal Register*, Vol. 43, No. 166, 1978, pp. 38295–38309.

Ergometrics and Applied Personnel Research, Inc., *FireTEAM Validation Report*, Lynnwood, Wash.: Ergometrics Inc., 2004.

Gottfredson, Linda S., "Skills Gaps, Not Tests, Make Racial Proportionality Impossible," *Psychology, Public Policy, and Law*, Vol. 6, No. 1, 2000, p. 129.

Groves, Robert M., Floyd J. Fowler, Jr., Mick P. Couper, James M. Lepkowski, Eleanor Singer, and Roger Tourangeau, *Survey Methodology*, Hoboken, N.J.: John Wiley & Sons, 2004.

Haddad, Abigail, Kate Giglio, Kirsten Keller, and Nelson Lim, *Increasing Organizational Diversity in 21st-Century Policing: Lessons from the U. S. Military*, Santa Monica, Calif.: RAND Corporation, OP-385 (from the Military Leadership Diversity Commission, July 2009 to March 2011), 2012. As of November 17, 2014: http://www.rand.org/pubs/occasional_papers/OP385.html

Hardison, Chaitra M., "Work Samples," in Steven G. Rogelberg, ed., *Encyclopedia of Industrial and Organizational Psychology*, Thousand Oaks, Calif.: Sage Publications, 2007.

Hardison, Chaitra M., Carra S. Sims, and Eunice C. Wong, *The Air Force Officer Qualifying Test: Validity, Fairness, and Bias*, Santa Monica, Calif.: RAND Corporation, TR-744-AF, 2010. As of November 17, 2014: http://www.rand.org/pubs/technical_reports/TR744.html

Hardison, Chaitra M., Carra S. Sims, Farhana Ali, Andres Villamizar, Benjamin F. Mundell, and Paul Howe, *Cross-Cultural Skills for Deployed Air Force Personnel: Defining Cross-Cultural Performance*, Santa Monica, Calif.: RAND Corporation, MG-811-AF, 2009. As of November 17, 2014: http://www.rand.org/pubs/monographs/MG811.html

Hardison, Chaitra M., and Anna-Marie Vilamovska, *The Collegiate Learning Assessment: Setting Standards for Performance at a College or University*, Santa Monica, Calif.: RAND Corporation, TR-663-CAE, 2009. As of November 17, 2014: http://www.rand.org/pubs/technical_reports/TR663.html

Hardison, Chaitra M., and Paul R. Sackett, "Kriterienbezogene validität des assessment centers: Lebendig und wohlauf? [Assessment Center Criterion-Related Validity: Alive and Well?]," in H. Schuler, ed., *Assessment Center zur Potenzialanalyse [Assessment Center for the Analysis of Potential]*, Göttingen, Germany: Hogrefe, 2007, pp. 192–202.

Hough, Leaetta M., and Frederick L. Oswald, "Personnel Selection: Looking Toward the Future—Remembering the Past," *Annual Review of Psychology,* Vol. 51, No. 1, 2000, pp. 631–664.

Hulett, Denise M., Marc Bendick, Jr., Sheila Y. Thomas, and Francine Moccio, "Enhancing Women's Inclusion in Firefighting in the USA," *International Journal of Diversity in Organisations, Communities & Nations*, Vol. 8, No. 2, 2008, pp. 189–207.

I/O Solutions, "Technical Report: Development and Validation of the National Firefighter Selection Inventory," 2010.

International Association of Fire Chiefs, "New CPAT Licensing Requirements," web page, March 1, 2009. As of July 3, 2014: http://www.iafc.org/Operations/LegacyArticleDetail.cfm?ItemNumber=3299

Judge, Timothy A., Joyce E. Bono, Remus Ilies, and Megan W. Gerhardt. "Personality and Leadership: A Qualitative and Quantitative Review," *Journal of Applied Psychology*, Vol. 87, No. 4, 2002, p. 765.

Lim, Nelson, Abigail Haddad, and Lindsay Daugherty, *Implementation of the DoD Diversity and Inclusion Strategic Plan: A Framework for Change Through Accountability*, Santa Monica, Calif.: RAND Corporation, RR-333-OSD, 2013. As of November 17, 2014:
http://www.rand.org/pubs/research_reports/RR333.html

Lim, Nelson, Carl F. Matthies, Greg Ridgeway, and Brian Gifford, *To Protect and To Serve: Enhancing the Efficiency of LAPD Recruiting*, Santa Monica, Calif.: RAND Corporation, MG-881-RMPF, 2009. As of July 3, 2014:
http://www.rand.org/pubs/monographs/MG881.html

Lloyd, Jonathan, "Mayor Orders Halt to 'Fatally Flawed' LAFD Recruitment Process: The Nonprofit RAND Corporation Will Review the Department's Recruiting Process and Make Recommendations," NBC Los Angeles, March 21, 2014, online edition. As of June 12, 2014:
http://www.nbclosangeles.com/news/local/LAFD-Fire-Department-Hiring-Recruitment-Process-Mayor-Eric-Garcetti-251298311.html

Lopez, Robert J., and Ben Welsh, "Eric Garcetti Scraps LAFD Hiring Process, Says It's 'Fatally Flawed'," *Los Angeles Times*, March 30, 2014a.

Lopez, Robert J., and Ben Welsh, "LAFD Recruit Program Is Suspended," *Los Angeles Times*, March 30, 2014b.

Lopez, Robert J., David Zahniser, and Ben Welsh, "Two L.A. Fire Commanders Reassigned," *Los Angeles Times*, February 28, 2014.

Manacapilli, Thomas, Carl F. Matthies, Louis W. Miller, Paul Howe, P. J. Perez, Chaitra M. Hardison, Hugh G. Massey, Jerald Greenberg, Christopher Beighley, and Carra S. Sims, *Reducing Attrition in Selected Air Force Training Pipelines*, Santa Monica, Calif.: RAND Corporation, TR-955-AF, 2012. As of November 17, 2014:
http://www.rand.org/pubs/technical_reports/TR955.html

Marquis, Jefferson P., Nelson Lim, Lynn M. Scott, Margaret C. Harrell, and Jennifer Kavanagh, *Managing Diversity in Corporate America: An Exploratory Analysis*, Santa Monica, Calif.: RAND Corporation, OP-206-RC, 2007. As of November 17, 2014:
http://www.rand.org/pubs/occasional_papers/OP206.html

Matthies, Carl, Nelson Lim, and Kirsten Keller, *Identifying Barriers to Diversity in Law Enforcement Agencies*, Santa Monica, Calif.: RAND Corporation, OP-370, 2012. As of November 17, 2014:
http://www.rand.org/pubs/occasional_papers/OP370.html

Newman, Daniel A., and Julie S. Lyon, "Recruitment Efforts to Reduce Adverse Impact: Targeted Recruiting for Personality, Cognitive Ability, and Diversity," *Journal of Applied Psychology*, Vol. 94, No. 2, March 2009, pp. 298–317.

Ones, Deniz S., Chockalingam Viswesvaran, and Frank L. Schmidt, "Comprehensive Meta-Analysis of Integrity Test Validities: Findings and Implications for Personnel Selection and Theories of Job Performance," *Journal of Applied Psychology*, Vol. 78, No. 4, 1993, p. 679.

Orlov, Rick, "Los Angeles Mayor Eric Garcetti Stops Los Angeles Fire Department Recruiting, Hiring," *Daily News* (Los Angeles), March 20, 2014, online edition. As of June 12, 2014:
http://www.dailynews.com/government-and-politics/20140320/
los-angeles-mayor-eric-garcetti-stops-los-angeles-fire-department-recruiting-hiring

Peresie, Jennifer L. "Toward a Coherent Test for Disparate Impact Discrimination," *Indiana Law Journal*, Vol. 84, No. 3, 2009, p. 1.

Ployhart, Robert E., and Brian C. Holtz. "The Diversity-Validity Dilemma: Strategies for Reducing Racioethnic and Sex Subgroup Differences and Adverse Impact in Selection," *Personnel Psychology*, Vol. 61, No. 1, 2008, pp. 153–172.

Principles—See Society for Industrial and Organizational Psychology, Inc., *Principles for the Validation and Use of Personnel Selection Procedures,* fourth edition, Ohio: Bowling Green, 2003.

Ridgeway, Greg, Nelson Lim, Brian Gifford, Christopher Koper, Carl F. Matthies, Sara Hajiamiri, and Alexis K. Huynh, *Strategies for Improving Officer Recruitment in the San Diego Police Department,* Santa Monica, Calif.: RAND Corporation, MG-724-SDPD, 2008. As of July 3, 2014:
http://www.rand.org/pubs/monographs/MG724.html

Robinson, Gail, and Kathleen Dechant, "Building a Business Case for Diversity," *The Academy of Management Executive*, Vol. 11, No. 3, 1997, pp. 21–31.

Roth, Philip L., Craig A. Bevier, Philip Bobko, Fred S. Switzer, and Peggy Tyler, "Ethnic Group Differences in Cognitive Ability in Employment and Educational Settings: A Meta-Analysis," *Personnel Psychology*, Vol. 54, No. 2, 2001, pp. 297–330.

Ryan, Ann Marie, Robert E. Ployhart, and Lisa A. Friedel, "Using Personality Testing to Reduce Adverse Impact: A Cautionary Note," *Journal of Applied Psychology*, Vol. 83, No. 2, 1998, p. 298.

Sackett, Paul R., Chaitra M. Hardison, and Michael J. Cullen, "On Interpreting Stereotype Threat as Accounting for African American–White Differences on Cognitive Tests," *American Psychologist*, Vol. 59, 2004, pp. 7–13.

Sackett, Paul R., Neal Schmitt, Jill E. Ellingson, and Melissa B. Kabin, "High-Stakes Testing in Employment, Credentialing, and Higher Education: Prospects in a Post-Affirmative-Action World," *American Psychologist*, Vol. 56, No. 4, 2001, p. 302.

Salgado, Jesus F., Chockalingam Viswesvaran, and Deniz S. Ones, "Predictors Used for Personnel Selection: An Overview of Constructs," *Handbook of Industrial, Work & Organizational Psychology, Volume 1: Personnel Psychology*, 2001, p. 165.

Schmidt, Frank L., and John E. Hunter, "The Validity and Utility of Selection Methods in Personnel Psychology: Practical and Theoretical Implications of 85 Years of Research Findings," *Psychological Bulletin*, Vol. 124, No. 2, 1998, p. 262.

Schmitt, Neal, and David Chan, *Personnel Selection: A Theoretical Approach*, Thousand Oaks, Calif.: Sage Publications, 1998.

Sims, Carra S., Chaitra M Hardison, Maria C. Lytell, Abby Robyn, Eunice C. Wong, and Erin N. Gerbec, *Strength Testing in the Air Force: Current Processes and Suggestions for Improvements*, Santa Monica, Calif.: RAND Corporation, RR-471-AF, 2014. As of December 2014: http://www.rand.org/pubs/research_reports/RR471.html

Smither, James W., Richard R. Reilly, Roger E. Millsap, Kenneth Pearlman, and Ronald W. Stoffey, "Applicant Reactions to Selection Procedures," *Personnel Psychology*, Vol. 46, No. 1, 1993, pp. 49–76.

Society for Industrial and Organizational Psychology, Inc., *Principles for the Validation and Use of Personnel Selection Procedures,* fourth edition, Ohio: Bowling Green, 2003. As of May 9, 2014: http://www.siop.org/_principles/principles.pdf

Standards—*See* American Educational Research Association, American Psychological Association, National Council on Measurement in Education, and Joint Committee on Standards for Educational and Psychological Testing, *Standards for Educational and Psychological Testing*, 2014.

Triandis, Harry C., Lois L. Kurowski, and Michele J. Gelfand, "Workplace Diversity," 1994.

Truxillo, Donald M., Dirk D. Steiner, and Stephen W. Gilliland, "The Importance of Organizational Justice in Personnel Selection: Defining When Selection Fairness Really Matters," *International Journal of Selection and Assessment*, Vol. 12, Nos. 1–2, 2004, pp. 39–53.

Truxillo, Donald M., Todd E. Bodner, Marilena Bertolino, Talya N. Bauer, and Clayton A. Yonce, "Effects of Explanations on Applicant Reactions: A Meta-Analytic Review," *International Journal of Selection and Assessment*, Vol. 17, No. 4, 2009, pp. 346–361.

U.S. Census Bureau, Profile of General Population and Housing Characteristics: Los Angeles County, 2010. 2010 Demographic Profile.

Welsh, Ben, and Robert J. Lopez, "Complete Guide to the LAFD Hiring Controversy," *Los Angeles Times*, April 20, 2014.